Mobile Phones for Language Learning in Japanese Universities

A book for university language students and teachers

Shudong Wang

Fueisha

Preface

The mobile phone, now generally understood as the smartphone in most cases, is in the possession of almost every university student in Japan. These tertiary students use the smartphone to make phone calls, take pictures, check information, and entertain themselves. Many students may also use the mobile phone to assist their learning, especially to assist them in language learning. Looking up new words and doing their language homework on mobile phones is now a norm for many students. How can students effectively use the mobile phone for learning languages; which function of the mobile phone is suitable for which skill training, i.e. vocabulary, listening, reading, speaking, or writing? What are students' concerns when they conduct mobile language learning? What language learning content do Japanese university students prefer for studying on their mobile phones? What are their leaning habits/preferences when they actively learn using their mobile phones?

No matter whether you are a teacher or a learner, you will find the answers to the above questions in this book. The book is a collection of research papers on mobile language learning published in various academic journals, many of which are high level ones indexed in the Web of Science with high impact factors. The author of the book holds degrees in English language education and in educational technology. He has been enthusiastically researching and practicing mobile language learning for more than ten years based on his work in three Japanese universities located in the Chugoku Region.

Funded by the Ministry of Education, Culture, Sports Science and Technology of Japan, as well as Shimane University, in cooperation with his colleagues, the author has implemented several mobile language learning projects. Thousands of students who studied with these projects reported that the projects were helpful and significant. Thanks are due to the students, and their participation and involvement - the feedback has brought the writer a huge data bank from which he is able to see with insight the successes and challenges of mobile language learning.

Gratitude also goes to his co-authors and project colleagues. These include: Douglas Jarrell, Professor of Nagoya Women's University; Jun Iwata, Professor of the Medical School, Shimane University; Simon Smith, Lecturer of Queen's University, Belfast, UK; Neil Heffernan, Professor of Kurume University. Special thanks go to Jim Kable, a retired teacher from the former Tokyo University of Science in Yamaguchi (now the Sanyo-Onoda City University), who has variously offered editorial advice. And he would also like to express his thanks to his Head of Department, Professor Hirose Kozo, who gave much support to his idea of carrying out mobile language learning projects with the students of Shimane University.

Finally, the writer is offering here a free mobile app for learning English developed himself. Download it to your smartphone and start to experience mobile language learning now!

iPhone/iPad download   Android download

Table of Contents

Preface ·· i

Chapter 1. What Is Mobile Language Learning? ·········· 1

1.1. Mobile Phones in Readiness for Mobile Learning 1

1.2. Mobile Language Learning - the Most Practiced Mobile
Learning 3

1.3. Background of Using Mobile Phones for Language Learning –
Mobile 2.0 Era 6

1.4. Possible Use of Mobile Phones for Language Learning 14

References 19

**Chapter 2. Present Practices of Mobile Language
Learning in Japanese Universities** ··· 26

2.1. Listening and Vocabulary via Mobile Phones 26

2.2. Reading and Grammar on Mobile Phones 28

*2.2.1. A Mobile Reading and Grammar Project at Shimane
University* 28

2.2.2. Reading on Mobile Phones: Motivation Counts 47

2.2.3. Conclusion 51

References 52

2.3. Mobile Language Learning Content Development 61

2.3.1. Introduction 61

2.3.2. Feasibility of Involving Students in Mobile Learning Content Development 64

2.3.3. Method 68

2.3.4. Results 72

2.3.5. Successes 77

2.3.6. Challenges 78

2.3.7. Conclusion 80

References 81

2.4. Mobile Language Learning Styles of Japanese Students 84

2.4.1. Introduction 84

2.4.2. A mobile assisted language learning project 86

2.4.3. Mobile learning features seen from Japanese project participants 90

2.4.4. Students' preferences on mobile learning materials 92

2.4.5. Students' attitudes toward student-created mobile learning materials 96

2.4.6. Student preferred mobile learning time 97

2.4.7. Students' motivation of participating in mobile learning 98

References 100

Chapter 3. Exploring Japanese Students' Mobile Language Learning Habits ⋯⋯⋯⋯⋯⋯⋯⋯⋯⋯⋯⋯ 102

3.1. Introduction 102

3.2. Research Purposes 105

3.3. Method 108

3.4. Data Results	110
3.5. Discussion	119
3.6. Conclusion	122
References	124

Chapter 4. Security, Privacy and Copyright Issues of Mobile Language Learning 127

4.1. Security 127

4.2. Online Privacy: Perceptions of Students 128

4.2.1. Introduction 128

4.2.2. Method 128

4.2.3. Results 130

4.2.4. Discussion 138

4.2.5. Conclusion 144

4.2.6. Research limitations 145

References 146

4.3. Copyright and Multimedia Classroom Material for Mobile

Language Learning: A Study from Japan 150

4.3.1. Introduction 150

4.3.2. Research purposes 151

4.3.3 Methods and techniques 158

4.3.4. Results data analysis 159

4.3.5. Discussion and conclusion 169

4.3.6. Proposed solutions 170

References 173

Chapter 5. Future Mobile Language Learning with VR and AR 179

5.1. What is VR? 179

5.2. What is AR? 180

5.3. AR/VR for General Educational Purpose 181

5.4. AR/VR for Foreign Language Learning on Mobile Phones 185

5.5. Problems and Limitations of VR and AR for Foreign Language Learning 189

5.6. Conclusion 190

Reference 191

Author Profile 193

Chapter 1

What Is Mobile Language Learning?

1.1. Mobile Phones in Readiness for Mobile Learning

In the last two decades, mobile technology has witnessed incredible development: from analog to digital and from plain and simple feature phones to the current 4G, LTE and incoming 5G smartphones which can serve as a mini-computers, telephones, radios, televisions, cameras and many other tools. This rise in technology has been so monumental that it is outpacing the devices that are currently on the market.

In Japan, NTT Docomo launched world's first mobile Internet-services platform in 1999. Twenty years later, Japan is still a country that has one of the world's most advanced cellular networks. In Japanese universities, almost the entire student population possesses smartphones. In part due to the ubiquity of Wi-Fi and WiMAX, price reduction of mobile data, smartphone users have become the norm rather than the exception. Smartphones connecting to Wi-Fi or WiMAX have the same connectivity as computers. Even in the current 3G and 4G environment, the data processing capability of phones gives users far greater flexibility than ever before. The change is not just limited to the wireless environment, mobile phone hardware has seen exponential progress as well. The screen size of some smart phones has increased to five inches or larger and the resolution has improved to around 2436*1125 pixels. The processing power of mobile phone CPUs also continues to evolve, and the memory cards on smart phones can store dozens of gigabytes of data, comparable with many PCs. It is clear that the gap in the operational functionalities between mobile phone and PC technology has narrowed, providing educators greater freedom for extending learning outside of traditional learning environments. While some limitations for mobile phone use in education existed in the past (Wang & Higgins, 2005), these have begun to dissipate due to advances in information technology. For instance, the problem of small bandwidth has been remedied by the technologies of Wi-Fi, WiMax, 3G, 4G and LTE networks. Similarly, problems associated with manual text input are being resolved through the use of speech recognition technology, touch screens, and styluses. Since the emergence of smartphones in 2007, more and more functions specific to PCs and other hand-held devices have been integrated within mobile phone devices.

In Japan, most mobile phones are now equipped with photo and video cameras, Quick Response (QR) code readers, voice recorders, MP3/MP4 players and some are equipped with 1seg technology, which allows for mobile reception of terrestrial television, Global Positioning System (GPS), Internet access, email, Short Messaging Service (SMS) and Multimedia Messaging Service (MMS). Applications of social media such as YouTube, LINE, Facebook, Skype, Twitter, Flash-embed or Java-enabled multimedia resources are all

Chapter 1

accessible on mobile phones. In addition, there are numerous smartphone apps are available in iTunes and Google Play Store for students to download for specific purposes. In sum: today's digital environment has blurred the differential between mobile phones and PCs.

1.2. Mobile Language Learning - the Most Practiced Mobile Learning

Technology is never absent in education. This is not only because education is a big market for technology, but also because teachers are always looking for suitable technology to assist their teaching. Another impetus for teachers to use technology for their classes may come from their students, a group of young men who are always enthusiastically using newly emerged technologies in their daily life. They push their teachers to embrace new technology.

Mobile handsets such as smartphones, tablet PCs, iPad, IC-recorders, iPods, MP3 players and digital dictionaries are now widely used in educational settings around the world. Mobile learning, is defined by Wikipedia as "learning across multiple contexts, through social and content interactions, using personal electronic devices". In terms of using mobile devices to learn languages, it is called Mobile Language Learning or Mobile Assisted Language Learning. In this book, we unified it as mobile language learning.

Mobile language learning focuses on the mobility of the language learner, interacting with portable technologies. Using mobile

3

tools for creating language learning aids, for example software and materials becomes a very important part of informal learning. Mobile language learning is convenient in that learners can learn a language from virtually anywhere like trains, buses, stations or of course at home, at any time such as waiting for friends, bus arrival and flight departure. Mobility is the biggest difference of mobile language learning from the other forms of learning, such learning with computers, or learning with paper materials, or learning in fixed classrooms.

As the price of smartphones continues to fall, they have ceased to be a tool of an elite minority. Almost 100% of Japanese university students now own personal smartphones, providing a possibility for mobile language learning. Whilst we cannot presuppose that such numbers will translate to a high number of mobile language learners, predictions for high future correlations do seem likely. For example, Cheon, Lee, Crooks, and Song (2012) indicate that college students in America are beginning to accept mobile learning. Similarly, in Japan, a majority of Japanese students surveyed by Thornton and Houser (2005) preferred to receive learning materials on mobile phones rather than PCs. Current pedagogical theory also shows a parallel enthusiasm for mobile learning. Situated Learning Theory (SLT) maintains that genuine learning is unintentional and situated within authentic activity, context, and culture. Discussing the effectiveness of mobile assisted language learning, Burston (2011) asserts that behaviorist, teacher-centered theories can complement and aid student-centered vocabulary and grammar mobile phone applications. Collaborative, learner-centered pedagogical approaches have undoubtedly informed and inspired developments in mobile learning programs. Language learning via mobile phones are becoming widely used in learning vocabulary, as is shown in a number of studies (Kennedy & Levy, 2008; Lu, 2008; Pincas, 2004; Stockwell, 2008; Stockwell, 2010; Thornton & Houser, 2005; Yamaguchi, 2005). In one study, Lu (2008) had students learn two sets of English vocabulary words either through mobile phones or by a paper-based format. Students who learned via SMS were found to understand more words than students presented with the paper-based tasks. Kennedy and Levy's (2008) research investigated the acceptability of a pushed mode of mobile phone operation; these authors sent short messages containing known words and new words mixed together. They found that the students appreciated the experience of reviewing learnt information and that the students found the message content often useful or enjoyable. Despite the challenge of integrating mobile phones into a learning environment, it has been shown that as users become more adept at using digital interfaces, their learning styles and how they perceive the learning material are both likely to change (Stockwell, 2010). Delivering smaller modular chunks—such as miniessays and grammar quizzes—may be more suitable for better mobile phone learning experiences. Indeed, academics (Rutherford, 1987; Krashen, 1989) have long suggested that acquisition is enhanced when learnt in comprehensible, manageable pieces. With this in mind—and in order to address an absence of data on the development of reading and grammar skills via mobile phones—Wang & Smith (2013) initiated a project in 2009, providing students with English reading and grammar learning materials in small modular chunks.

Since the majority of mobile language learning activities are conducted through mobile phones, this book specifically focuses its attention on mobile phones for language learning.

1.3. Background of Using Mobile Phones for Language Learning – Mobile 2.0 Era

The notion of Mobile 2.0, which essentially, is Web 2.0 on mobile handsets, and the implications for language learning. In this book, we are primarily concerned with mobile phones, the most commonly carried and used handheld device. There are many other handheld devices which have the potential to supply language learners with the opportunity to learn ubiquitously, such as Personal Digital Assistants (PDAs), smartphones, MP3/MP4 players, iPods, IC-recorders/players, portable radios, tablet PCs, portable DVD players, and digital dictionaries. However, with the ever-improving development of mobile phone technologies, the dividing line between mobile phones and computers is becoming blurred, and it will soon be difficult to differentiate between them, as mobile phones will be able to build on most of the functions of these other devices.

Technology acts to mediate communication (Sharples, 2000, p.

Chapter 1

183), with communication now being the focal point of the teaching methods used by language teachers worldwide. Mobile learning is regarded as the new generation of learning (Levy & Stockwell, 2006), and with the establishment of the mobile learning pedagogical theory (Ogata & Yano, 2004), in many countries, some open universities have already successfully conducted mobile learning in distance learning education programs, and the results have proven to be effective (Thornton & Houser, 2004, McCarty, Obari, & Sato, 2017).

Japanese university students use mobile phones when commuting to and from school, during intervals between classes, before and after dinner, and when they relax at home. To this end, a survey of Japan National Federation of University Co-operative Associations (2014) shows that Japanese university students spend 3 hours on their mobile phones each day. In the same survey, 63% of the respondents said they would like to use mobile phones for language learning.

Despite the globalization of the telecommunications business, some human behavior is still local. Japanese university-aged students use their mobile phones for any number of functions, and tend to carry them with them everywhere they go. In addition, the use of emails, SNS via mobile phones enhances sociability among university students (Ishii, 2004), which has clear implications for the manner in which these students live their lives and their resultant expectations in terms of their communication habits. To be precise, young Japanese people tend to use their mobile phones for socialization and for text-based communication with their friends and classmates (Ito, 2004). As a result, the cultural trends and needs of Japanese university students auger well for mobile-based language teaching.

Thus, there is no doubt that mobile phones have great potential for language learning. From a pedagogical viewpoint, mobile assisted language learning is often associated with an informal learning setting which can take place whenever the learners want it to happen. Language learning appears to be a good candidate for learning in informal settings (Hoppe, 2007).

Why mobile phone is suitable for language learning? The first advantage is that it provides timely teaching feedback. Mobile 2.0 has seen the development of language learning topics, language tips, and even textbooks and teaching plans that can be ranked and commented on via mobile phones. Since mobile phones are highly accessible, the feedback from students for their teacher's products can occur quite quickly and accurately. Mobile devices used for language learning should act as the learner's assistant rather than teacher (Sharples, 2000), and should offer the opportunity for an interface with which to interact in a meaningful way for language learners.

Mobile phone users tend to carry their phones with them everywhere they go and have access to them all day long. For the purposes of learning languages, PC users can only have access to learning materials when they are in front of their computers. For this reason, learners can only gain access to lesson content or evaluate

Chapter 1

their teachers when they get online in school or at home. This prevents the students from giving timely feedback on the teacher's lesson immediately after class when they have the lesson content fresh in their minds. Mobile 2.0 changes this in a remarkable way. If learners can use an evaluation system that is based on their mobile phones, then feedback can be collected accurately and quickly without any extra burden on the learner.

To this end, Maeda, Okamoto, Miura, Fukushige and Asada (2007) formulated a survey which can be used for evaluating teaching based on the mobile phone's email function. The system proved to be more effective than PC and paper evaluations commonly conducted by language teachers and learners. In Maeda et al.'s mobile email-based system, students are asked to view an online questionnaire with several multiple-choice questions and comment boxes to investigate their attitudes toward the class they just attended. As every student had a mobile phone with Internet capability, the survey had a very high rate of effective responses (Maeda, et al., 2007).

The second advantage is real-time alerts. In a world of PC Web 2.0, people need to sign into their accounts to generate Web 2.0 content such as blogs, SNS and share photos and videos. After that, content developers (users) must wait for others to view their messages or choose to subscribe to new ones through RSS feeds. The problem with this method is that in order to perform all these functions, users must be near a PC. This is not a restriction for Mobile 2.0 users, as they can send updated information to subscribers via mobile-based alert systems, which can be accessed in real-time.

Mobile 2.0 can also spread information more effectively than Web 2.0 by utilizing existing SNS platforms. SMS used to be the text major communication tool between mobile phones users, now replaced by email or SNS like Line. Still, email is universally available for Japanese mobile phones (Mobile White Book, 2007), and mobile phone holders can still be reached by PC email accounts.

Kogure et al. (2007) and Thornton and Houser's (2005) surveys indicated that 99% of Japanese university use their phones to send and receive emails. What is more important to educators in Kogure et al.'s (2007) survey is the fact that 89% of Japanese university students use their mobile phone email function more than their PC email function. This trend continues to 2017 and 2018 and confirmed by other newly conducted surveys by the author of this book. Thus, the ubiquitous nature of mobile phones, and the desire for students to use them frequently creates great potential for language learners and teachers alike.

The term MALL (Mobile Assisted Language Learning) was coined by Chinnery (2006), who regarded digital handsets such as mobile phones, PDAs and iPods as useful tools for language learning. He cited several language learning projects using mobile phones, including ones by Stanford Learning Lab, which gives Spanish learners access to vocabulary, quizzes and live talking tutors, all via their mobile phones. Second, Thornton and Houser (2003) tested short English lessons with their learners by sending

Chapter 1

them mobile phone email addresses. Levy and Kennedy (2005) used the SMS function on mobile phones to assist students in learning Italian. All of the results of these programs were reported to be effective for language learning (Chinnery, 2006). These projects are believed to be the pioneer projects in mobile assisted language learning in the world.

However, all of the above programs were developed before the concept of mobile 2.0 became as popular at it is now. In these programs, learners could interact within the program to a certain extent, but the interaction was not really user-led. Likewise, the essential features of mobile 2.0 are its user-led, community-based and collaborative content. Similarly, language learning on mobile phones must emulate this type of interaction in order to best serve the needs of learners.

What is Mobile 2.0? O'Reilly Media created the phrase Web 2.0 in 2004 to refer to a supposed second-coming of the web that allowed users to collaborate and share information online in new ways by using web technologies such as CSS (Cascading Style Sheets), SOAP (Simple Object Access Protocol), REST (Representational State Transfer), XHTML, Ajax (Asynchronous JavaScript and XML), mashups, RSS and tagging. The concept of Web 2.0 is essentially a transition from the online consumer to the consumer/producer/participant. Podcasting, blogs, SNS, Second Life, wikis and YouTube are all examples of Web 2.0 that have been enthusiastically researched and used for language learning purposes (Thomas,

2007a, 2007b). However, what will happen if Web 2.0 for the PC world is extended to mobile handsets?

Mobile 2.0, or Mobile Web 2.0 (Jaokar & Fish, 2006), refers to the extension of Web 2.0 to mobile devices, and specifically to mobile phones. Mobile 2.0 is a term that has been used since the appearance of Web 2.0 in 2004. Since then, educators started using terms such as 2.0 to refer to applications that have innovations stemming from Web 2.0 technologies, like CALL 2.0 (Computer Assisted Language Learning), MALL 2.0, and Learning 2.0 (McCarty, 2007). Mobile 2.0 can be understood as extending the idea of Web 2.0 to mobile devices; the mobile version of Web 2.0.

Mobile 2.0 constitutes the next generation of transferring data to mobile devices and it links Web 2.0 with the mobile platform to create something new: it creates a new set of services that has greatly increased mobility and is as easy to use as the Web. These services point the way forward for the mobile data industry (Appelquist, 2006, para. 21). This demonstrates the pace at which this emerging field of research and learning is moving. Furthermore, some researchers argue that Mobile 2.0 is outpacing the speed and form of Web 2.0, because the former is not limited by time and location constraints (Miyazawa, 2006).

One of the major advantages of mobile learning is that it is spontaneous, portable and very personal to the user. Further, it can also be informal, unobtrusive and ubiquitous (Kukulaska-Hulme & Traxler, 2005). The following section will propose, examine and

Chapter 1

prove the efficacy of Mobile 2.0 when it is integrated with language learning and teaching.

In the first half of 2004, SNS providers simply transferred their services from PCs to mobile phones without considering the special features of mobile phones. From the winter of 2004 to 2005, Japanese providers using SNS started to embed mobile phones with unique functions like GPS and mobile games. Coupled with these, Mobile social software can facilitate social encounters by allowing users to see others who are in the same geographic location as them. The implications for language learning are clear: Mobile 2.0 users can easily find out who in their community is nearby and available to talk and/or learn simultaneously.

Mobile SNS integrated with online games is another new tendency in Mobile 2.0. One successful integration of SNS and online games in Japan can be found at Mobage-town <http://mbga.jp>, a free mobile site offering free online games and a wide variety of community functions such as blogs, email, chat, and message boards. The site had some English games on it that can be used by language learners to gain a different perspective on language learning. After all, language teachers often employed games in their classrooms, so extending them to mobile phone usage is another facet of Mobile 2.0 that can greatly assist the language learner.

Mobile 2.0 users are ubiquitously involved in content editing. In schools, language teachers can encourage students to write or film their blogs or edit class wikis in the target language. Mobile communication can significantly increase students' extrinsic motivation without increasing the pressure on language learners.

1.4. Possible Use of Mobile Phones for Language Learning

Some technologies are best suited for particular language learning activities. For example, the SMS function on mobile phones used to be ideal for vocabulary learning as vocabulary items are naturally short and can be easily segmented into small, individual definitions and examples (Levy & Kennedy, 2005). A similar situation exists with the nexus between Mobile 2.0 and language learning. For example, text blogs are helpful for training writing ability and improving social identity (Thorne & Payne, 2005; Chiao, 2006). Wikis are useful for promoting collaborative language writing. Thorne and Payne (2005) cite some educational projects utilizing Wiki technologies for language learning. L.Wiki (a particular Wiki to support Unicode encoding), supported by Pennsylvania State's national foreign language resource center is used by a variety of groups and language courses, including Chinese, German, Russian, Spanish, English composition, and also for English as a Second Language courses.

In the case of podcasts (an episodic series of digital audio or video files which a learner can download and listen to) for language listening, it is worth noting that podcasting-assisted English learning programs started in April, 2004 at Osaka Jogakuin College,

Chapter 1

Japan (McCarty, 2005). 15-gigabyte iPods were provided to 210 newly enrolled freshmen. These iPods came installed with audio materials designed to improve learners' listening abilities. Since 2009, Hiroshima University has being creating podcasting materials (Sealwood, Lauer & Enokita, 2015) covering various topics which are thought to interest Japanese university students. The project is welcomed by the students and is still going on. Some other language podcasts such as BBC six minutes podcasts, VOA Podcast are also very popular in Japanese university language classes.

Do-it-yourself: Mobile 2.0 sites for language learning. A popular and free Mobile 2.0 site builder for language teaching can be found at Winksite <http://winksite.com>. The site claims that it makes it easy to create mobile Websites and communities that can be viewed worldwide on any mobile phone. Winksite allows users to build their own blogs, chat forums, conduct polls and create journals. It is truly user-friendly in that it does not require the user to download or install any software, and allows users to build and manage a mobile community over which they have total control (Winksite, 2019).

Language teachers can easily avail themselves of Winksite's functions. For example, teachers can make announcements to students, post homework assignments, give quizzes, and discuss language tasks assigned in previous lessons. The use of mobile phones for these activities offers a multitude of educational opportunities for language learners, as it promotes interactivity and gives them quick and easy access to discussion and timely feedback from teachers (Thornton & Houser, 2003). Furthermore, teachers can encourage learners to work collaboratively on writing assignments in the target language (TL), read magazines, and conduct group work, all via their mobile phones by customizing services from this site (see Figure 1).

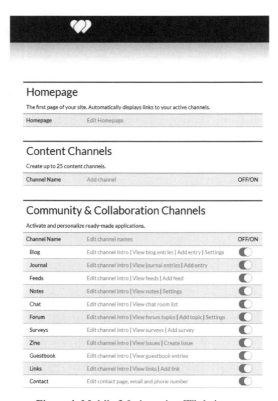

Figure 1. Mobile 2.0 site using Winksite

Chapter 1

Foreign language acquisition through mobile blogs, SNS and games. Beginning with mixi <http://mixi.jp>, which was extremely popular around 2004 in Japan once had 4 million registers and 130 million page views (PV) per day. Another popular blog site in Japan, Livedoor, had 8.6 million registered users by the end of April, 2006 (Mobile White Book, 2007). Both sites could be accessed by mobile phones, with both having a large contingency of foreign community users. Japanese language learners using these mobile sites had access to everyday Japanese language use at their fingertips. The same can be said for learners of English, as there are a large number of English speaking bloggers belonging to these sites who regularly read and comment on the blogs on the sites. Access to these blogs gives foreign language learners yet another study option for learning the.

SMS integrated with instant messengers (IM). SMS for language learning had been gaining in popularity before SNS emerged. Levy and Kennedy (2005) sent Italian words, idioms and example sentences to students' mobile phones as SMS messages. The project proved successful for aiding in language learning and demonstrated that the use of SMS in language learning is a pedagogically sound technique.

Instant messengers (IM) are also valuable tool for language learners. According to Warschauer (1997), time and place-independent communication is one of the fundamental tenets of CALL, indicating that using movable instant messengers, like SMS, has the potential to greatly enhance a learners' experience with the TL. The integration of SMS and IM, which is advancing in the Mobile 2.0 world, serves as a connection between mobile phone users and PC users. Moreover, it connects mobile phone users even closely to each other, giving them an advantage over conventional PC users. In China, people can send instante messages to mobile phones using QQ or Wechat, the most popular instant messengers with Chinese youth. Instant messengers like Skype and Line were available on most mobile phones with Internet capabilities, and mobile phone users can easily enter communities like mobile blogs from their phones. Users can chat online with mobile phones partners or PC users. This allows potential language learners to exchange information much more conveniently when they are on the move.

Li and Erben (2007) report that language learners are capable of increasing their intercultural awareness with prolonged use of instant messenger services. They argue that these services can assist in boosting self-reflection capacities, critical thinking skills and create a greater sensitivity and respect for intercultural differences. In a time and age when these skills are so important for survival in an increasingly globalized world, language teachers and learners cannot afford to overlook the benefits of acquiring these qualities.

GPS for context aware language learning. GPS navigation service allows people to find out a precise physical location with a high degree of accuracy. In Japan, GPS functions have been widely built into mobile phones. Educators can use this function with their

Chapter 1

learners to get them to work as a team and to make language learning more context-aware.

For example, language learners can use this function to search for other users who are near their current location. A smartphone application using GPS makes it much easier for language learners to find a friend who is interested in creating a learning group with similar interests.

Mobile LMS/ CMS for language learning. LMS (Learning Management Systems) or CMS (Course Management Systems) are complex software or platforms designed for planning and managing learning activities online or offline. Moodle, a free open source teaching and learning management platform, and Blackboard (WebCT), a widely used commercial LMS. Gyuto-e and ALC NetAcademy are good examples of LMS used for language learning purposes in Japan. Of many which are accessible from mobile phones.

CMS technology has been much improved in recent years. WordPress, Moodle, Sitecore, Joomla and Drupal has many mobile phone oriented themes available to download and their content can be automatically adjusted to fit small screens.

References

Appelquist, D. (2006). What is mobile 2.0? Retrieved October 2, 2007, from: http://www.torgo.com/blog/2006/09/what-is-mobile-20.html.

Burston, J. (2011). Exploiting the Pedagogical Potential of MALL,

In Proceedings of Mobile Learning as the future of education. San Sebastián, Spain. Retrieved April 26, 2019, from https://www.researchgate.net/publication/258962305_Exploiting_the_pedagogical_potential_of_MALL

Cheon J., Lee S., Crooks S., Song, J. (2012). An investigation of mobile learning readiness in higher education based on the theory of planned behavior, *Computers & Education, Vol. 59(3)*, 1054-1064.

Chinnery, G. (2006). Emerging Technologies: Going to the MALL. Mobile Assisted Language Learning. Language Learning & Technology, 10(1), 9-16. Retrieved April 25, 2019, from: http://llt.msu.edu/vol10num1/emerging/default.html

Chiao, T. (2006). Applications of blogging in an EFL writing class: A case study. Paper presented at the JALT CALL 2006 Conference in Sapporo, Japan.

Hoppe, U. (2007). How can we integrate mobile devices with broader educational scenarios? Big issues in mobile learning: Report of a workshop by the Kaleidoscope Network of excellence mobile learning initiative. Nottingham, UK: The University of Nottingham.

Houser, C., & Thornton, P. (2004). Japanese college students typing speed on mobile devices. Proceedings of second IEEE workshop on wireless technologies in education (WMTE 04), 129-133.

Houser C., & Thornton, P. (2005). Poodle: A course-management system for mobile phones. Proceedings of the third IEEE workshop on wireless technologies in education (WMTE 05), 159-163.

Ishii, K. (2004). Internet use via mobile phone in Japan. Telecommunications Policy 28, 4358.

Ito, M. (2004). Personal Portable Pedestrian: Lessons from Japanese Mobile Phone Use. Paper presented at Mobile Communication and Social Change, the 2004 International Conference on Mobile Communication in Seoul, Korea. Retrieved on April 25, 2019, from: www.itofisher.com/mito/archives/ito.ppp.pdf

Jaokar, A. & Fish, T. (2006). Mobile Web 2.0: The innovator's guide to developing and marketing next generation wireless/mobile applications. London: Futuretext Limited.

Kennedy, C., & Levy, M. (2008). L'italiano al telefonio: Using SMS to support beginners' language learning. *ReCALL, 20(2)*, 141–161.

Kogure, Y., Shimoyama, Y., Anzai, Y., Kimura, M., Goda, Y., & Handa, J. (2007). A study of the mobile phone market for mobile learning, Proceedings of the 23rd Annual Conference of Japan Society of Educational Technology (pp. 53-56). Tokyo: JSET.

Kozaki, Y. & Nishii, Y. (2006). The mechanism of mobile phones. Tokyo: Niike Soft Press.

Kukulaska-hulme, A., & Traxler, J. (2005). Mobile teaching and learning. In Kukulaska-hulme, A., & Traxler, J. (Eds.), Mobile Learning: A Handbook for Educators and Trainers (pp. 25-43). London: Taylor & Francis.

Sealwood, J., Lauer, S. & Enokida. K (2015). What are more effective in English classrooms: textbooks or podcasts? 2015 *Eurocall* Proceedings, 424-428.

Levy, M. (2003). Effectiveness of CALL technologies: finding the right balance. In R. Donaldson & M. Haggstrom (Eds.), Changing language education through CALL. Lisse: Swets & Zeitlinger.

Levy, M., & Kennedy, C. (2005). Learning Italian via mobile SMS. In Kukulska-Hulme & J. Traxler (Eds.), Mobile Learning: a handbook for educators and trainers.76-83. London: Taylor & Francis.

Levy, M., & Stockwell, G. (2006). CALL dimensions: Options and issues in computer assisted language learning. N. J.: Lawrence Erlbaum Associates, Inc.

Li. J. & Erben T. (2007). Intercultural learning via instant messenger interaction. CALICO Journal 24(2), 291-231.

Maeda, T., Okamoto, T., Miura, T., Fukushige, Y., & Asada, T. (2007). E-mail-based education environment using mobile phone communication. Proceedings of the 7th IEEE International Conference on Advanced Learning Technologies, Niigata, Japan, 427-429.

McCarty, S. (2005). Spoken Internet to Go: Popularization through Podcasting. *The JALT CALL Journal 1(2)*, 67-74.

McCarty, S. (2007). Web 2.0 Technologies for research and mobility. In M. Thomas (Ed.), Wireless Ready e-Proceedings:

Podcasting Education and mobile assisted language learning, Nagoya Japan, 13-32. Retrieved May 10, 2007, from: http://wirelessready.nucba.ac.jp/eproceedings.html

McCarty, S., Obari, H. & Sato, T. (2017). *Implementing Mobile Language Learning Technologies in Japan*. Singapore: Springer

Miyazawa Y. (2006). Mobile 2.0: Business on mobile devices in the times of post Web 2.0. Tokyo: Impress, Co., Ltd.

Mobile White Book. (2007). Tokyo: Impress R&D.

Ogata, H., & Yano, Y. (2004). Knowledge awareness pap for computer-supported ubiquitous language-learning. In J. Roschelle, T. W. Chan, & S. J. H. Yang (Eds.), Proceedings of the 2nd IEEE International Workshop on Wireless and Mobile Technologies in Education (p. 19). Los Alamitos, CA: IEEE Computer Society.

Sharples, M. (2000). The design of personal mobile technologies for lifelong learning. *Computers and Education 34*, 177-193.

Stockwell, G. (2007). Vocabulary on the move: Investigating an intelligent mobile phone-based vocabulary tutor. Computer Assisted Language Learning 20(4), 365-383.

Thorne S. & Payne J. (2005). Evolutionary Trajectories, Internet-mediated Expression, and Language Education. *CALICO Journal, 22(3)*, 371-397.

Thornton, P., & Houser, C. (2003). Adding interactivity to large lecture classes in Japan via mobile phones. In D. Lassner & C. McNaught (Eds.), World Conference on Educational Multimedia, Hypermedia and Telecommunications (pp.1871-1874).

Chesapeake, VA: EDMEDIA.

Thornton, P. & Houser, C. (2004). Using mobile phones in education. In J. Roschelle, T. W. Chan, & S. J. H. Yang (Eds.), Proceedings of the 2nd IEEE International Workshop on Wireless and Mobile Technologies in Education (pp. 3-10). Los Alamitos, CA: IEEE Computer Society.

Thornton, P., & Houser, C. (2005). Using mobile phones in English education in Japan. *Journal of Computer Assisted Learning 21(3)*, 217-228.

Thomas, M. (2007a). An introduction to wireless ready: ready or not? In M. Thomas (Ed.), Wireless Ready e-Proceedings: Podcasting Education and mobile assisted language learning, Nagoya Japan. Retrieved April 25, 2019, from: http://wirelessready.nucba.ac.jp/eproceedings.html

Thomas, M. (2007b, June). Student produced podcasts with Garage-Band: A business English presentation course case study. Paper presented at JALTCALL 2007 Conference, 2007, Tokyo.

Tsutsumu, Y., & Yuyichi, K. (2005). Mobile certified examination. Tokyo: Ritoshoyin.

Wang, S. & Higgins, M. (2005). Limitations of mobile phone learning. *Proceedings of IEEE International Workshop on Wireless and Mobile Technologies in Education*, 179-181.

Warschauer, M. (1997). Computer-mediated collaborative learning: Theory and practice. Retrieved April 25, 2019, from: https://pdfs.semanticscholar.org/171c/69f6d24129207424a9ad9e154e

Chapter 1

ed28c39b08.pdfl

Weippl, E. (2005). Security and trust in mobile multimedia. In I. K. Ibrahim (Ed.). Handbook of mobile multimedia (pp. 22-34). NY: Idea Group Reference.

Winksite (2017). Retrieved October 13, 2007, from: http://winksite. com

Yamaguchi, T. (2005). Vocabulary learning with a mobile phone. *Program of the 10th Anniversary Conference of Pan-Pacific Association of Applied Linguistics*. Edinburgh, UK.

Chapter 2

Present Practices of Mobile Language Learning in Japanese Universities

2.1. Listening and Vocabulary via Mobile Phones

Learning vocabulary through the medium of mobile phones is now a widely practiced and well-established method of teaching. (Lu, 2008; Chen & Chung 2008; Kennedy & Levy, 2008; Thornton & Houser, 2001; Yamaguchi, 2005; Pincas, 2004). In one study, Lu (2008) had students learn two sets of English vocabulary either through mobile phones or by a paper-based format. Students who learned via mobile short message service (SMS) were found to comprehend more vocabulary than when presented with a paper-based format. Kennedy and Levy's (2008) research investigated the acceptability of a 'push' mode of mobile phone operation by sending short messages containing known words and new words, and found that the students appreciated the experience of reviewing learnt information overall, as well as finding the message content often useful or enjoyable. Butgereit & Botha (2009) described a system that allows the language teacher to create spelling lists or vocabulary lists in English and Afrikaans. The system then generates a fun mobile phone application using multiple texts-to-speech engines to encourage African pupils to practice spelling the words. Cavus, & Ibrahim (2009) developed a system to send technical

Chapter 2

English language words together with the meanings in the form of Short Service Messages (SMS).

MALL practice is not limited to vocabulary; research also shows that cultural understanding can also be deepened by mobile blogs. Comas-Quinn, & Mardomingo (2009) carried out a mobile learning project to engage learners in the creation of an online resource that focuses on the foreign culture. In their project, students could use their mobile phones, digital cameras and MP3 recorders to select and record samples of their encounter with the foreign cultures, and then send them or upload them to the cultural blog to share with the group. Chang & Hsu (2011) developed a system to integrate an instant translation mode, an instant translation annotation mode, and an instant multi-users shared translation annotation function to support a synchronously intensive reading course in the normal classroom. This MALL project was designed for PDAs, not for mobile phones. Demouy & Kukulska-Hulme (2010) reported a project that let students use iPODs and MP3 players, as wells as mobile phones to practice listening and speaking. They found that the use of iPods and MP3 players was quickly adopted by project participants; but whilst the challenge and the authenticity of doing activities on the mobile phones were less satisfying.

2.2. Reading and Grammar on Mobile Phones

2.2.1. A Mobile Reading and Grammar Project at Shimane University

Compared with mobile phone vocabulary learning and practices with listening and speaking, there is significantly less research on the advantages of mobile phone programs for reading and grammar practice. Waycott and Kukulska-Hulme (2003) reported that students found it difficult to read course materials on a PDA (a mobile device that is not popular with university students in Japan) and that it was generally considered to be inferior to reading in a paper-based format. Lan, Sung, and Chang (2007) explored the potential of mobile technology for reading, but their experiment was limited to tablet PCs and their participant pool only included elementary school students. The research of Huang and Lin (2011) shows that in terms of reading, receiving materials on paper is preferable to receiving resources via mobile phones or email regardless of the length of the texts. Whilst this is an important finding, the study only involved 10 students; furthermore, the study based its findings on the reading of just six texts. In addition to the shortage of research into mobile reading and grammar learning, another important factor which inspired this project is the popularity of mobile phone novels in Japanese. Kawaharazuka and Takeuchi (2010) and Farrar (2009) reported that by 2007, five of the best-selling print novels in Japan were written and read on mobile phones. The prevalence for reading novels on phones was interpreted as a positive indication that

Chapter 2

students would look favorably on this current project if some of the protocols of writing novels were also adopted for the project. This included frequent use of the line return and the use of short sentences with few modifiers. With these factors in mind we wanted to provide students with a learning opportunity that would help improve their English and allow us to have a better understanding of reading and grammar learning on mobile phones while also giving us the opportunity to assess the degree to which students are motivated to learn outside the classroom on their mobile phones. For these reasons we started a project called "Ubiquitous English" in 2009. To fully immerse students in a rich learning environment, short English essays and grammar quizzes were sent to students via their mobile phones two or three times a week. Students were then required to complete the activities on their mobile phones in their own time. During the course of our three-year project, several questions came up repeatedly and became a motivating force for the study. These questions include:

1. Are students prepared to read a foreign language and engage with grammar quizzes on their mobile phones? When students read on mobile phones, what kinds of topics motivate and what kinds of topics fail to captivate their interest?

2. When given the choice between accessing material on mobiles or PCs, which device will students instinctively use?

3. What general perception do students have towards reading and grammar on mobile phones?

4. What concerns do students have about learning languages using their mobile phones?

By addressing these questions, this section aims to redress the gap in current research into mobile learning for reading and grammar practice as well as inform future research of important observations regarding this specific student population.

The initial reading materials used within this project were developed by university teachers from the Center for Foreign Language Education, Shimane University, Japan. In order to enhance and extend the program, 10 advanced-level students were temporarily employed to write essays that were to be read by our students. These materials were uploaded by the students and later edited by university teachers. The task of writing short essays, however, was predominantly assigned to the native English-speaking teachers. At the outset of the project, it was agreed that each composition would be no more than 140 words in length, so that each essay could be read in two or three minutes on a small screen (Borau, Ullrich, Feng, & Shen, 2009; Grosseck & Holotesch, 2008). In order to appeal to a majority of first-year students, whose average knowledge of English is at a pre-intermediate level, all the materials were written in simple and easy-to-understand English. Any words that we thought might cause a problem were picked out and given a note in Japanese.

Furthermore, having learning materials created for learners by a teacher who is familiar with the students' learning needs is more likely to resonate positively with the students, enhance their

Chapter 2

classroomobile learning, and hopefully, increase their motivation towards language learning. Also, from a teaching perspective, creating in-house materials enables teachers to offer material which learners themselves see as relevant and applicable to other situation (Ngeow, 1998). This is also reflected in earlier research on motivation. In one such study, Oxford and Shearin (1994) analysed 12 motivational theories and identified six factors that affect motivation in language learning. One of the factors highlighted was "environmental support," which is defined as the "extent of teacher and peer support, and the integration of cultural and outside-of class support into learning experience." In order to appeal to our young participants, the topics chosen for the mobile learning project were as topical and broad-based as possible. To capture student interest, the topics chosen were not overly taxing and included jokes and riddles. Although listening skills had never been the focus of this project, we were aware that reading accompanied by pictures and audio is always more effective than a text-only format (Fiorea, Cuevasa, & Oserb, 2003; Glenberg & Langston, 1992.). Accordingly, since August 2011, all materials in our project have included both audio and visual content to support the readings. Students could then listen to or watch each reading (see essay example in Figure 1, above, and the MP4 formatted animation in Figure 1, below).

```
                    Ghost Town
Notes:
national news 全国ニュース;
scare 恐怖;
torch 懐中電灯;
creepy 気味の悪い;
-----------
Matsue is popular for many reasons: its natural beauty, its
history and its local traditions. However, recently Matsue
hit national news because of a new attraction - ghosts.
According to the Japan Times, a ghost tour has become a
popular attraction for people looking for some adventure and
scares. The tour has participants carry torches and visit
graveyards in the middle of the night. The tour visits places
referred to in horror stories from the Meiji novelist Yakumo
Koizumi. Leading it is his great-grandson who seems to share
his great-grandfather's interest in creepy places. (Written
by Simon Smith)
Reading quiz: What do the participants do on the tour?
-----------
▼For a Japanese translation and answer to the reading quiz
click on the following links
https://ixl.inter-scc.jp/ic/e?i=eTbAWo0CaYc&m=1
▼Animation for this essay:
https://ixl.inter-scc.jp/ic/e?i=eTbAWo0CaYc&m=1
▼Feedback on today's essay:
https://ixl.inter-scc.jp/ic/e?i=eTbAWo0CaYc&m=1
```

Figure 1. Mini essay (above) and an MP4 formatted animation for this mini essay (below)

Chapter 2

Alongside the reading text, which was usually a short story, a joke or an anecdote, two types of grammar materials were provided: grammar knowledge and grammar quizzes. In a previous e-learning program, we had discovered that most students at our university are typically weak at using nouns, the subjunctive mood, participles, and negative forms. To address these areas, the grammar interpretations sent to students focused on these items. Each grammar item interpretation was attached with a grammar quiz URL. From a project objective, the grammar knowledge delivery was a form of explicit teaching (i.e., Figure 1. Mini essay and an MP4 formatted animation for this mini essay, pushing student learning) whereas the grammar quiz was seen as a test of their understanding (i.e., pulling student learning). Sometimes trivia associated with English grammar were added to the grammar activities in order to increase students' motivation. Because most of the readers were first-year students at the pre-intermediate level, part of the grammar section was written in Japanese (see Figure 2).

Figure 2. Grammar explanation sent via email (left) and grammar quiz (right)

Grammar explanation sent via email (left) and grammar quiz (right). Because the learning materials were mainly delivered via email, our first priority was to obtain students' email addresses. As personal information is strictly protected by Japanese law (The Cabinet Office of Japanese Government, 2005), students were under no obligation to provide teachers with their email addresses (El-Khatib, Korba & Yee, 2003; Kimura, Komatsu, Shimagawa, Shirahase, & Sekine, 2005). Thus, after distributing handouts to every first-year student, we explained the goal of our project and the purpose of requesting their email addresses. Students were asked to register their email addresses of their own volition and were told that their

Chapter 2

email address would be used only for this project. They were also told they could opt out at any time. Upon beginning the project, we were aware that many students might be reluctant to share their personal information with an e-learning system (Boston, 2009; Wang & Heffernan, 2010), so we consented to the use of nicknames when students registered their email addresses. In total, as of June 2012, 372 email addresses had been registered with the project. Unfortunately, not all of the registrants became permanent participants, reducing the number of active participants to 208. There were four predominant reasons for the loss of so many subscribers: (a) some students found the program unsuitable for their learning style and chose to terminate their subscription; (b) Japanese students frequently change their mobile phone email addresses in order to avoid spam emails, and some forgot to update this information with the project; (c) many students' mobile phones are pre-set by telecommunication companies to prevent receiving emails from PCs; and (d) the emails from the project server were automatically filtered to the spam folder.

Once created, the reading and grammar materials were uploaded to the server. These were sent to students through the server's email system as an email in plain text with the URLs attached. The email system was set to send out 20 emails per minute in plain text to lower the possibility that the learning materials be blocked as spam or be treated as suspicious. For every reading text, a simple comprehension exercise was designed to check student understanding.

Grammar quizzes were then sent via URLs attached to each grammar point review (see Figure 3). When students opened their email, the reading materials could be read as messages, so students did not need to go beyond the link provided. A comment/quiz system was used for the purpose of student-teacher interaction. All of these systems were designed or customized for mobile phones, but were also compatible with any PC. URL links contained Japanese translation notes, material rank interfaces, and grammar quizzes. Figure 4 indicates the information flow throughout the project.

Figure 3. Quiz interaction with score and explanation

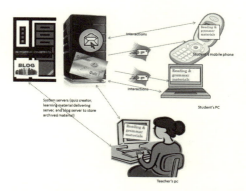

Figure 4. Technical work flow of mobile learning material delivery

Registration for the project was always open-ended, but students who joined the project at later dates could not access earlier readings. For these students, a blog system was built to store archived material for the students to browse. We archived all materials that were sent out via emails in web format by using the open-source content management system, WordPress. The web site was customized for use on mobile phones. Between June 2010 and June 2013, the archived mobile phone blog site logged 68,166 page views.

The data from the project feedback were collected using the following methods: online surveys, server log analysis, and interviews. Three consecutive web surveys written in Japanese were conducted among the subscribers in 2010, 2011, 2012, 2013 and 2014. The data presented in this section is from the latest survey conducted in April 2012. The survey's URL was sent by email to students and was accompanied by the survey's rationale and questions. Students were informed that their identity would remain anonymous, and furthermore, that they were under no obligation to complete the questionnaire. As the questionnaire was delivered to their mobile phones, we limited it to eight short questions. Seven were multiple-choice questions, and the last one was an open-ended question asking their general opinion about the project (see Appendix). The survey was available online for two weeks from April 2nd to April 16th. The survey questions were grouped into three categories: Questions 1, 5, 6, and 7 investigated which materials students like to read on mobile phones. Question 2 asked about the type of digital learning device that was used to receive materials. Questions 3 and 4 surveyed students' overall perceptions of the project. Half of the questions from the survey asked for the students' assessment of the learning materials. This is because according to Day and Bamfors' Expectancy and Value Model (1998), good material development is one key factor in motivating students to read in foreign languages. It is only when the materials engage the students, (i.e., easy to read, short, with interesting content) that they feel motivated to continue learning (Takase, 2003). Fifty-six project participants answered the questionnaire (n = 56) which represents a response rate of approximately 27%. Whilst the somewhat low response rate does not automatically indicate that the survey was inaccurate or unrepresentative (Taylor, Drummond, & Strang, 1997; Holbrook, Krosnick, & Alison, 2007), data from other project records—a server data analysis and interviews—were

Chapter 2

used to support the results from the questionnaire. Technically, the system could not detect whether the learning materials sent in plain text via email were read or not. However, the number of clicks on the automatically generated URLs attached to the emails was recorded by the server. The system recorded who took the quiz and when the quiz was taken, as well as any score details. For the archived materials stored on the blog site, the system could also track IP addresses, as well as store the information on the type of material that was accessed. Two types of participants were selected to be interviewed. The first type consisted of users who registered from the onset of the program until the close of the study; the second type included students who joined the program but withdrew after only a short period of participation. In total, four students—two males and two females who were all randomly chosen from those who registered with their real names—were interviewed after class on separate days. During the interview each user was asked why he or she chose to continue with or leave the project.

The first question asked respondents about their attitude towards the learning materials developed by their peers, referring to the learning materials developed by 10 students recruited from within the university. Out of 56 respondents, 36 (64%) said they enjoyed the essays as well as some of the grammar quizzes written by students. The remaining 20 (36%) indicated their indifference by selecting the neutral option. This is a clear indication that the majority of students welcome reading and learning materials developed by their peers. In terms of student-created materials, we also analyzed feedback from our server logs. This was possible because for each message sent, subscribers were invited to leave comments. Whenever the learning materials were sent out, we included the author's name so that readers could identify the author of the material. On average, the learning materials developed by native English-speaking teachers received three comments each. Interestingly, this number increased on average to five when the materials were written by students (and corrected by teachers). When quizzes were created by students, the average number of students taking part in quizzes also increased from 20 to 25. Whilst the data is not statistically significant ($t = 2.33$, $p < .05$), comments from users were very positive as demonstrated below:

This is a good try. Actually I didn't realize the essay was written by my schoolmate until I saw the author's name.

It feels intimate to read essays written by ourselves, about ourselves and for ourselves. Can I also contribute my essays?

These comments show that mobile reading and grammar materials created by students probably increases motivation to read. Furthermore, despite not being "authentic" (i.e., published, native-English authored) texts, they were by no means regarded as inferior by students. Rather, the appeal or approval probably came from the fact that the writing comes from the students, themselves. For future developments in mobile learning materials, extensive involvement of students in mobile learning material development is worth considering.

Chapter 2

Questions 5 and 6 were designed to examine which materials were rated the highest. English essays (41%), trivia (34%), and grammar quizzes (27%) were ranked as the most read/accessed materials. Seven percent of students surveyed ranked "all materials" as the most read, and the same percentage of students said that "none" were their most read. The results imply that rather than taking grammar quizzes, students prefer to read essays and trivia surrounding language. The fact that essays are preferred to grammar quizzes should remind us that materials read or interacted with on mobile phones should not be too demanding. In terms of the different essay genres, these have been ranked below in decreasing order of preference: English jokes and riddles (45%), cultural differences (30%), life/living/entertainment (27%), and topics related to the environment (12.5%) and proverbs (12.5%). Unpopular topics included English learning methodology (5%), science and technology (4%), society (4%), and politics (4%). Our findings from the ranking of essay topics demonstrate that learning through interesting materials, (i.e., English jokes and riddles), or something more esoteric, (i.e., cultural differences, or campus life) can best attract students' attention and provide stimulation for any project.

Question 7 asked students to rate the suitability of the learning materials used in the project according to their own English level/needs. Sixty-three percent thought that the level of writing was suitable; whilst 37% indicated that they thought the materials were difficult. From this we can state that materials developed by teachers

41

and peers are well suited for and viewed favorably by students. In addition to the above information, we also looked at the access logs of our web materials using a WordPress plugin called Visitor Map. This took a snapshot of the daily traffic between June 1 and June 10, 2012. The number of times each essay was accessed is presented below.

Table 1. Web Access to the Mobile Reading and Grammar Materials

	Topics	Accesses	Percentage
Essays	Cultural differences	76	21%
	Environment	22	6%
	Life/living/entertainment	41	11%
	English proverbs/ idioms/sayings/quotations	46	13%
	English learning techniques	16	4%
	Science and technology	5	1%
	Society	17	5%
	English jokes/riddles	62	17%
	Politics	2	1%
Grammar knowledge and quizzes		9	2%
Trivia of English (in Japanese)		69	19%
Total		365	100%

Note. The above accesses were all from Japanese IP addresses including the entries from Google search engine.

Chapter 2

As can be seen in Table 1, essays concerning cultural differences (21% of all accesses) and English jokes/riddles remained the most popular topics among readers. Web access data confirmed students' preferences for the materials identified by the survey.

Question 2 asked which device each student used for receiving the learning materials. Forty-one (73%) respondents reported that they used a mobile phone. Only 14 (25%) said they used their PC's email addresses for the project. Only one student reported using an iPad to receive the materials. The data is consistent with the email registration when recruiting subscribers for the project. Of the 372 subscribers, 279 (75%) students registered with their mobile phone, although they were told that PC email addresses were acceptable. This further illustrates the willingness and confidence that first-year students have towards using mobile phones for language learning. These results support the research findings of Thornton and Houser (2005). Furthermore, our results echo recently published figures that show a high use of mobile phones: indeed, 95.6 % of senior high school students in Japan possess mobile phones, of which 95.1% have Internet connection; of senior high school students, 75.6% use the Internet more than two hours every day (The Cabinet Office of Japanese Government, 2011). The same survey results show that first-year university students, typically 18 or 19 years old, have been using mobile phones for some years and have become adept at using them on many levels. This could explain why such a large proportion of our respondents (73%) reported that they used a mobile

43

phone to access the learning materials. Questions 3 and 4 investigated the overall perception of the project by the students.

Question 3 asked: How often do you read the learning materials? Forty students (71%) replied that they had read almost all of the materials, 11 (20%) said that they had read everything, and five (9%) indicated that although registered with the project, they had never read any of the content.

Question 4 asked if the project was helpful in improving their English reading and grammar ability. Forty (71%) reported positively, saying that they thought the project, in general, was helpful in developing their reading and grammar ability.

According to our questionnaire, the project was well-received by the students. As the project was not associated with any mandatory English course, students were free to opt out or disregard any of the learning materials. In spite of this, 20% indicated that they had read all the materials. Furthermore, 71% of participants felt that their reading and grammar abilities had improved by taking part in the project.

Ideally, the progress of subscribers' reading and grammar abilities should be assessed on a yearly basis. However, as stated earlier, the purpose of this project was to provide a relaxed reading and grammar practice environment for students. We also wanted to explore the impact of delivering informal reading and grammar exercises to mobile phones. As participation was voluntary, and students were not tied to any physical classrooms, any form of

Chapter 2

assessment would be a significant challenge. Assessing mobile learning outcomes may be difficult if learners cannot be brought together into a controlled testing environment (Wang & Higgins, 2006).

Finally, Question 8 was an open-ended question inviting general comments about the project, to which 26 respondents gave comments. Most students (71%) perceived reading short essays on mobile phones as a helpful tool towards improving their reading ability. The comments listed below represent the overall perception of the program:

I like the short essays and I thought that every essay was interesting.
Although I don't always have time to read the essays, I think it is a good chance for us to be exposed to English.
I am too busy to read all of the essays; however I do believe that this is a good way to come into contact with authentic English.
I like reading on mobile phones. Unlike reading on a PC, I can read anytime, anywhere.
The words in the essays are sometimes challenging but at the same time the essays are easy to understand. It is a good project!

These comments capture the students' opinion that reading on mobile phones increases their exposure to English. Participants indicated that they liked the mode of reading content delivered by phone. Interestingly, many also commented that they would prefer receiving the material in an ad hoc fashion as opposed to receiving them on specific days each week. One implication of this is that students do not want to make a commitment to study; therefore, receiving the material in a less predictable manner may provide a less formal quality to the program. Similarly many students commented favorably on the short and easy-to-understand format of the reading material. As feedback indicated that students were inclined towards topics on cultural differences, as well as jokes and proverbs. Native-speaker teachers integrated grammar and vocabulary components into those topics. Despite the popularity of the reading content, this did not extend to the grammar quizzes, which received less participation than some of the reading materials. On average, each grammar quiz had only 23 volunteer participants—roughly equating to 11% of the total number of active subscribers. In an interview with a student who was active for the whole project, we asked why he felt students were less favorable towards online quizzes. He answered:

> We are tired with so many classes and do not want to use our brains to think about quizzes after class. Taking quizzes is not like reading interesting essays; it is not enjoyable at all. In addition, our teachers are probably monitoring our performance. It would be embarrassing if I did poorly in the quiz. Therefore, unless it is made into a compulsory assignment, I don't want to do the grammar quizzes.

This remark implies that unless there is an element of compulsion to the program, students are reluctant to do anything overly demanding unless it is linked to their overall grade—even if it is delivered via mobile phones. The lesson here is that optional

Chapter 2

learning materials designed for mobile phones should not be too challenging: this may reflect the fact that students may also not have the time or the energy nor the tools to engage in study outside of class that is seen as too time-consuming.

2.2.2. Reading on Mobile Phones: Motivation Counts

Research suggests that on average, 76.6% of Japanese university students spend more than 30 minutes a day reading or sending messages on their mobile phones; and 79.5% spend more than 30 minutes browsing the Internet on their mobile phones (MyNavi Co. Ltd., 2012). If students were to engage in reading activities on their phone for just a small portion of this time, it could be inferred that measurable improvements in their reading ability could be attained. Given the high usage of mobile phones within the student population, it was assumed that this would translate favorably with regards to our program. However, we severely underestimated one very important factor: motivation. Whilst a significant amount of time is spent browsing or socializing on phones, that time is not likely to be easily relinquished to a less rewarding activity (phone or otherwise). Similarly, if learning of any variety is to be extended onto mobile phones, it must engage students on a level that can compete with free games and social media—a formidable challenge. As we have noted, given the strong association between phones and gaming, motivating students to use their phone for learning is an ambitious task. This is compounded by the fact that reading in another

47

language is one of the hardest skills to acquire, as it requires higher-level comprehension processes. Therefore, the hard work needed to gain even modest improvement is perhaps the reason why many learners find reading one of the most challenging tasks among the four skills (Ngeow, 1998). Huang (2006) recognizes that with L2 reading "learner motivation may be a concern" (p. 3), but one which should not impede the learning process. Huang also pointed out that one of the important factors to motivate reading in an L2 is that teachers are available to answer questions. This offers possibilities for future innovations in mobile learning such as the integration of Mobile Instant Messaging. In the case of a class activity, reading a text under a teacher's supervision is obligatory and students are required to answer any questions posed by the teacher. However, for this project, registration was voluntary, as was the reading of essays or taking quizzes. Unlike formalized class study, there were no tests or formal evaluations of the subscribers. Students who entered this project did so of their own volition and with their own agenda. This appears to have lowered the participation. Only those students who already possessed high motivation or directed their study towards a goal-related purpose such as a job or study abroad program remained very active in the project. A future challenge for this project would be how to attract new membership but, most importantly, how to maintain student motivation. Many registered students left the project due to a lack of motivation connected to either material or extraneous factors. The activity of reading project material may in some

Chapter 2

way compete with or take away socializing or gaming time from students. Thus, firstly, an important aspect of any mobile reading project must be to devise ways to enhance the motivation for reading English content. Secondly, some form of incentive may need to be offered in order to compete with the already high demands of social networks and games on the mobile phone. We interviewed a student who participated in the project for all of 2010 but quit in 2011. Our question was: Why did you choose to join the program in the beginning and what caused you to quit? He replied:

In the beginning I thought it was compulsory to read the essays.

I also thought that some questions in the mid-term or final exams might be included in the learning materials that the project sent. However, I discovered that this was not the case. In fact the learning materials sent to my mobile had nothing to do with the academic credits. The essays are indeed interesting and informative, but just doing homework from regular English classes is enough. I don't have extra energy and time to read on my mobile phone. I also heard that many of my classmates did not join the project and they were not affected at all, so I decided to quit too.

This view may represent a majority of other students who may not want to read and practice English on their mobile phones. No matter how good the reading material is, these students will not be motivated by mobile reading unless:

1. Learning outcomes are linked with a specific course goal and/or that the students' performance is eventually evaluated or recog-

nized through course credit.

2. Learning progress and performance are formally monitored. Students need to have assurances that they are in a social arena with their teachers or peers.

3. There is some recalibration of the material during the project to reflect the comments and feedback of students. This can be maintained through close monitoring of the server logs and comments from the students.

The concept of mobile phone learning, although not yet prevalent, is likely to become accepted by more and more learners. However, the disadvantages of mobile phone learning are still significant. As stated above, students are not used to reading learning materials on small screens. Taking quizzes or answering reading questions requires them to scroll up and down; interaction on mobile phones is not as easy as on PCs; and most importantly, students view mobile phones as their private domain which should remain disconnected from formal study. The distinction is clear: many students accept the concept that learning should be done in class or on a PC, whereas mobile phones are for their personal affairs. Changing this perception may require a shift in thinking as well as teaching. Indeed, given the high ownership rate of mobile phones, it is surprising that university students rarely use the mobile phone as an educational tool. In 2012, on our registration page, we asked the question: "Have you ever used mobile-phone for learning?" Sixty-two students (59%) said they have never used their phone for learning.

Chapter 2

Another factor obtained from the feedback is a concern about security, an issue to be disscussed in Chapter 4.

2.2.3. Conclusion

Although quantitative assessments were not carried out on a yearly basis, objective data were collected throughout the project in various ways: through registration records, quiz results, comments and the learning history stored on the server. The data combined with the results of interviews lead to the following conclusions: in general, mobile phone-assisted learning is perceived positively by students as an effective method for improving reading and grammar ability. But for learning to take place, the material must engage the learner, without being too demanding. For young university students, reading topics that focus on cultural differences and student life are the most relevant, as are jokes, and entertaining stories— which are regular favorites. Items such as grammar quizzes need to be kept to a minimum to avoid the perception of being seen as study. Security is always a big concern for mobile learners. Before launching a mobile learning project, Internet security should be carefully considered. This means that a secure learning platform, a secure mode for delivering learning materials, and a secure way to monitor students' progress should be in place. Our study also instructs us of the necessity to empower the students in some form of material development, as students themselves are best placed for knowing their own learning preferences. Additionally, mobile learning content is destined to be short and segmented. Our findings also highlight the importance of respecting a student's right to privacy. For a project to have any significant impact on learning outcomes, it must be highly responsive to any feedback—positive or negative. Finally, in order to compete with the ubiquity of games and social media, it may be necessary to offer students some form of inducement or incentive. We fully believe however, that having incentives is not the panacea, as learning should always bring its own reward. However, linking mobile learning to a formal course evaluation may be a crucial step to improving the efficacy of mobile learning.

We hope that this study will help focus the attention of other mobile learning practitioners to embrace a mobile phone learning culture. By working as partners with students, educational institutions can build an effective reading and grammar mobile program that places students at the forefront of learning.

(Sections 2.1 and 2.2 were originally published in *Language, Learning and Technology 17(3)*, with Simon Smith.)

References

Borau, K.,Ullrich,C.,Feng,J.,Shen. R.(200 9). Microblogging for language learning: using Twitter to train communicative and cultural competence. *Lecture Notes in Computer Science.Vol. 5686.* 78-87.

Boston, J. (2009). Social Presence, Self-Presentation, and Privacy in Tele-Collaboration: What Information Are Students Willing to

Share? *Journal of the Research Center for Educational Technology (RCET), Vol.5, No.3.* Retrieved June 21, 2012 from http://rcetj.org/index.php/rcetj/article/view/64/128

Burston, J. (2011). Exploiting the Pedagogical Potential of MALL, In *Proceedings of Mobile Learning as the future of education.* San Sebastián, Spain. Retrieved November 26, 2012, from http://www.moblang.m.obi/conference/files/PedagogicalAspects OfMobileLearning_MobLang_JackBurston.pdf

Butgereit, L., & Botha, A. (2009). Spelling vocabulary using a cell phone. In P. Cunningham & M. Cunningham (Eds.) *IST-Africa 2009 Conference Proceedings* ,1-7

Cabinet Office of Government of Japan. (2011). Survey result of Internet use of Japanese teen-agers. Retrieved December 26, 2012 from http://www8.cao.go.jp/youth/youth-harm/chousa/h23/net-jittai/pdf/kekka_g.pdf

Cavus, N., & Ibrahim, D. (2009). mobile learning: An experiment in using SMS to support learning new English language words. *British Journal of Educational Technology, 40(1)*, 78-91.

Chang, C-K., & Hsu, C-K. (2011). A mobile-assisted synchronously collaborative translation–annotation system for English as a foreign language (EFL) reading comprehension. *Computer Assisted Language Learning, 24(2)*, 155-180.

Chen, C-M., & Chung, C-J. (2008). Personalized mobile English vocabulary learning system based on item response theory and learning memory cycle. *Computers & Education, 51*, 624–645.

Cheon J., Lee S., Crooks S., Song, J. (2012). An investigation of mobile learning readiness in higher education based on the theory of planned behavior. *Computers & Education*, 59(2012) 1-54-1064

Comas-Quinn, A., & Mardomingo, R. (2009). Mobile blogs in language learning: making the most of informal and situated learning opportunities. *ReCall, 21(1)*, 96–112.

Day, R., & Bamford, J. (1998). Extensive reading in the second language classroom. Cambridge: Cambridge University Press.

Demouy, V., & Kukulska-Hulme, A. (2010). On the spot: Using mobile devices for listening and speaking practice on a French language programme. *The Journal of Open, Distance and e-Learning, 25(3)*, 217-232.

El-Khatib, K., Korba, L., & Yee, G. (2003). Privacy and security in e-learning. *Journal of Distance Education, 1, 4,* 1–16.

Farrar, L.(2009). Cell phone stories writing new chapter in print publishing, Retrieved June 23, 2012 from http://edition.cnn.com/2009/TECH/02/25/japan.mobilenovels/index.html

Fiorea, S., Cuevasa, H., & Oserb, R. (2003). A picture is worth a thousand connections: the facilitative effects of diagrams on mental model development and task performance. *Computers in Human Behavior, 19(2)*, 185–199;

Glenberg, M., & Langston, W.(1992). Comprehension of illustrated text: Pictures help to build mental models. *Journal of Memory and Language*. 31(2), 129–151

Grosseck, G., & Holotesch, C. (2008). Can we use Twitter for educational activities? Paper presented at the *Fourth International Scientific Conference eLearning and Software for Education*, Bucharest, Romania.

Heffernan, N., & Wang, S. (2008) Copyright and multimedia classroom material: A study from Japan, *The Journal of Computer Assisted Language Learning*. Vol.21 (2), 167-180.

Holbrook, Allyson., Krosnick, J., Alison, P. (2007). The causes and consequences of response rates in surveys by the news Media and government contractor survey research firms. In James M. Lepkowski, N. Clyde Tucker, J. Michael Brick, Edith D. De Leeuw, Lilli Japec, Paul J. Lavrakas, Michael W. Link, and Roberta L.(Eds.) *Advances in telephone survey methodology*. Sangster. New York: Wiley.

Huang,L., & Lin, C .(2011). EFL leaners' reading on mobile phones. *JALT CALL Journal*, *Vol.7 No.1*. 61-78.

Huang, S. (2006). Reading English for academic purposes –What situational factors may motivate learners to read? *System, 34*. 371-383

Kennedy, C., & Levy, M. (2008). L'italiano al telefonino: Using SMS to support beginners' language learning, *ReCALL, 20*. 315-330.

Kimura, T., Komatsu, Y., Shimagawa, S., Shirahase, F. & Sekine, M. (2005). *Nerawareru! Kojinyohou privacy higaikyousai no houritsu to jitsu [Personal data, privacy and their violation: law support and cases]*. Tokyo: Civil Law Research Association.

Kozaki, Y., & Nishii, Y. (2011). All about smart phones (in Japanese). *Nikkeibp: Tokyo*

Krashen, S. (1989). We acquire vocabulary and spelling by reading: Additional evidence for the input hypothesis. *Modern Language Journal, 73.* 440-464.

Kukulska-Hulme, A. & Shield, L. (2008). An overview of mobile assisted language learning: From content delivery to supported collaboration and interaction. *ReCALL, 20(3).* 271-289.

Lan, Y., Sung, Y., Chang, K. (2007). A mobile-device supported peer-assisted learning system for collaborative early EFL reading. *Language Learning and Technology, Volume 11, Number 3.* 130-151

Laufer, R. S., & Wolfe, M. (1977). Privacy as a concept and a social issue: a multidimensional developmental theory. *The Journal of Social Issues, 33,* 3. 22–42.

Levy, M., & Claire, K. (2005) Learning Italian via mobile SMS: In A. Kukulska-Hulme & J. Traxler (Eds.), *Mobile Learning: A Handbook for Educators and Trainers.* London: Taylor and Francis

Lu, M. (2008). Effectiveness of vocabulary learning via mobile phone. *Journal of Computer Assisted Learning, Volume 24, Issue 6,* 515–525

MyNabi Co. Ltd. (2012). Lifestyle survey on 2013 university graduates. Retrieved June 13, 2012 from http://saponet.mynavi.jp/

mynavienq/data/mynavienq_20120124.pdf.

Ngeow, K. (1998). Motivation and transfer in language learning. ERIC Digest. Retrieved December 27, 2012 from http://www.ericdigests.org/1999-4/motivation.htm

Oxford, R. & Shearin, J. (1994). Language learning motivation: Expanding the theoretical framework. *The Modern Language Journal*, *78(1).* 12-28.

Patricia, K., Irene. B., Stephanie, B., Stephanie, P., Terry, C. (2000). Book access, shared reading, and audio models: The effects of supporting the literacy learning of linguistically diverse students in school and at home. *Journal of Educational Psychology. Vol. 92(1).* 23-36.

Pincas A. (2004). Using mobile support for use of Greek during the Olympic Games 2004. In Proceedings of M-Learn Conference 2004. Rome, Italy.

Rutherford, W.(1987). Second language grammar: learning and teaching. New York: Longman. pp:181

Stockwell, G. (2007). Vocabulary on the move: Investigating an intelligent mobile phone-based vocabulary tutor. *Computer Assisted Language Learning, Vol.2, No. 4* 365-383.

Takase, A. (2003). Effects of eliminating some demotivating factors in reading English extensively in *JALT 2003 Shizuoka Conference Proceedings.* 95-103.

Taylor, D., Drummond, C. & Strang, C. (1997). Surveying general practitioners: does a low response rate matter? *The British Jour-*

nal of General Practice, 47(415). 91–94.

The Cabinet Office, Government of Japan (2005). Act on the protection of personal information. Retrieved June 18, 2012 from http://www.cas.go.jp/jp/seisaku/hourei/data/APPI.pdf

Thomos, K. (2011). Japanese students' experience of ICT and other technology prior to university: A survey. *JALT CALL Journal. Vol.7, No.1.* 93-102

Thornton, P., & Houser, C. (2001). Learning on the move: Vocabulary study via email and mobile phone SMS. In C. Montgomerie & J. Viteli (Eds.), *Proceedings of World Conference on Educational Multimedia, Hypermedia and Telecommunications,* 1896-1897. Chesapeake, VA: AACE.

Wang, S., & Heffernan, N. (2010). Ethical issues in Computer-Assisted Language Learning: Perceptions of teachers and learners. *British Journal of Educational Technology, Volume 41, Issue 5.* 796–813

Wang, S. & Higgins, M. (2005). Limitations of mobile phone learning. Proceedings: *IEEE International Workshop on Wireless and Mobile Technologies in Education,* 179-181.

Waycott, J., & Kukulska-Hulme, A. (2003). Students' experiences with PDAs for reading course materials. *Personal and Ubiquitous Computing, Volume 7, Number 1, DOI: 10.1007/s00779-002-0211-x,* 30-43.

Weisband, S. & Reinig, B. A. (1995). Managing user perception of email privacy. *Communications of the ACM, 38, 12.* 40–47.

Yamaguchi, T. (2005). Vocabulary learning with a mobile phone. *Program of the 10th Anniversary Conference of Pan-Pacific Association of Applied Linguistics*. Edinburgh, UK.

APPENDIX

Table 1. Survey on Reading and Grammar Study on Mobile Phones (n=56)

Options	%	Responses	Options	%	Responses
1. Between November 2011 and March 2012, 30 topics were developed by students, what did you think of these materials?			*2. What type of device did you usually receive the learning materials on for the project?*		
Good	64.3%	36	Ordinary model of mobile phone	44.6%	25
Neutral	35.7%	20	Smart phone	28.6%	16
Poor	0	0	PC	25.0%	14
Other	0	0	Other	1.8%	1
3. How often did you read the learning materials?			*4. Overall, do you think that this project was helpful in improving your reading and grammar ability?*		
All the time	19.6%	11	Very helpful	8.9%	5
Sometimes	71.4%	40	Somewhat helpful	62.5%	35
Never	8.9%	5	Neutral	25.0%	14
			Not very helpful	1.8	1
			Not helpful at all	1.8%	1
5. Which type of learning materials did you prefer?			*6. From the essays you read, what were your favorite topics?*		
Essays	41.1%	23	Environment	12.5%	7
Grammar quizzes	26.8%	15	Life/living/entertainment	26.8%	15
Trivia of English language	33.9%	19	Cultural differences	30.4%	17
All types	7.1%	4	English proverbs/idioms/sayings/quotations	12.5%	7
None	7.1%	4	English learning methodology	5.4%	3
			Science & technology	3.6%	2
			Society	3.6%	2
			Politics	3.6%	2
			English jokes/riddles	44.7%	25
7. Were the learning materials difficult?			*8. Any comments about the project are welcome.*		
Very difficult	3.6%	2			
Somewhat difficult	33.9%	19			
Appropriate	62.5%	35			
Somewhat easy	3.6%	2			
Very difficult	1.8%	1			

Chapter 2

2.3. Mobile Language Learning Content Development

2.3.1. Introduction

Mobile-assisted Language Learning (MALL) first became a reality as mobile devices, particularly cell phones, developed web connectivity at the beginning of the 21st century. The advent of phones with email or SMS capabilities was the first step towards mobile-assisted learning because it opened the way for content delivery. Any teacher could create content for reading and send it to multiple learners simultaneously. This differed from previous CALL (Computer Assisted Language Learning) where learners had to access a website and retrieve or "pull" the information. With email-capable cell phones, content could now be "pushed" to the learners wherever they were.

Some of the first pedagogical experiments with mobile learning, particularly in Japan, involved "pushing" content to learners' cell phones via email at regular intervals. This form of delivery was shown to be more effective in promoting retention of vocabulary in one project which compared it to online content delivery and the traditional paper delivery. Another study indicated that the use of mobile technology helped to sustain regular study among learners of Italian (Levy & Kennedy, 2005).

While there were initial concerns about the availability of mobile devices for students, the university student market for cell phones in Japan quickly approached saturation, with Thornton & Houser saying in 2002 that, "Educators in Japan can assume their

61

students will have recent hardware, and in particular, will carry mobile 'Internet phones' that can surf the Web and exchange email." (2002, pg. 231).

MALL has been receiving more and more attention with rapid technological advances in mobile phone hardware and wireless tele-communication networks. Many applications which used to be only available on PCs now have mobile versions, while MALL practices that used to be limited to vocabulary quizzes now are being extended to a variety of areas including reading, listening, cultural study, writing, and pronunciation training.

Vocabulary learning is one of the most common activities in MALL as can be seen in the large number of MALL vocabulary studies (Chen & Chung, 2008). Kennedy and Levy's (Kennedy & Levy, 2008) research investigated the acceptability of a pushed mode of mobile phone operation; these authors sent short messages containing known words and new words mixed together to students' cell phones. Cavus and Ibrahim developed a system to send out technical English language words together with their meanings in the form of SMSs (Cavus & Ibrahim, 2009). Obviously, the learning materials in these projects were created and sent out solely by teachers.

Web 2.0, or in case of mobile learning, Mobile 2.0, can be used as platforms for users to produce content. Podcasting, blogs, Wikis, WeChat, LINE, Second Life, and YouTube are all examples of Mobile 2.0 that have been enthusiastically adopted for language

Chapter 2

learning content development. Pinkman (2005) showed that peer reading and writing, as well as the interactive nature of blogs, can have a positive motivational effect on student writers. Pritchard (2008) also pointed to the motivating effect of writing for sites with user-generated content (UGC) such as Wikipedia. While these constructivist activities give learners the opportunity to practice the target language,, the content created by these learners may not be accurate enough for "push" content such as email magazines, which aim to provide both reading content and writing examples for learners.

University students these days have grown up as "digital natives" with Web 2.0 and Mobile 2.0, and are used to reading and writing short texts on mobile devices. Because of the screen size of mobile devices, mobile learning materials have tended to be short and focused, features that make these materials easier for students to cope with not only as readers and but also as creators.

So far, teachers and e-learning professionals have dominated the development of e-learning content with little student involvement. One study indicates that e-learning content development is regarded as expensive, time-consuming and complicated (Gümü, 2010). Ideally, teachers have ample funding and time to develop online materials. Unfortunately, the fact is, at least in Japan, that teachers are busy with face-to-face teaching and many other school obligations and responsibilities. At the same time, they are facing budget cuts every year. This generates the gap between what the teachers can afford to provide and what the students really need in terms of mobile learning content. This section aims to answer the following research questions:

1. Is it feasible to involve students, i.e., the learners themselves, in developing content for mobile learning?
2. Can students be motivated to develop mobile learning content for their own use?
3. Do the readers accept student-developed content and perceive it as equal to teacher-developed content?

2.3.2. Feasibility of Involving Students in Mobile Learning Content Development

Compared to PC based e-learning materials, such as PowerPoint slides, VOD (Video On Demand), and flash and other movie formats, mobile learning materials are usually in text or at their most complicated, in short audios or videos. This is one of the reasons we hypothesize that students are capable of developing such materials for mobile learning. At the same time, if students are given freedom to develop content that they like, the content will arouse interest in their peers. Finally, language teachers are usually too busy to create a large quantity of e-learning materials to store in a database for future use. Students may be able to fill this need for learning content. As student content developers are users at the same time, they should know what their cohorts are interested in and what their needs are, allowing them to create content that is more accessible.

Chapter 2

Teachers can shift from creating materials to supervising and assisting student content developers. To test these hypotheses, Shimane University and Nagoya Women's University, both universities in Japan, started a mobile learning project in 2013 that involved students in developing materials for an English email magazine targeting mobile phone users. In the first stage of the project, students were paid to write short essays, make grammar/vocabulary quizzes, and create learning animations. The second stage is calling for volunteer contributions from the several hundred current subscribers to maintain the project. The 2013 project is based on the following two pilot projects.

The Jaremaga Project

The Jaremaga Project began as an email magazine for extensive reading practice targeting the general public as well as university students. The university students who read the email magazine were English majors at a Japanese women's university studying in a curriculum that emphasized oral communication skills. Their TOEIC (Test of English for International Communication) scores and survey feedback indicated that reading was one of their weakest skills, so the daily email magazine was started to encourage regular reading practice.

Hamajima Shoten, a publisher of school workbooks, provided technical assistance to make a website so that learners could sign up for the email magazine. The company also set up an email server so that the messages could be sent out at a fixed time, 7:30 a.m., every morning. The texts were limited to approximately 80 words to make them readable on all the cell phones in use at the time. Topics covered a broad range, from cultural differences to the news of the day. The texts (hereafter called "essays") were purposely written in short sentences using simple English grammar. The readability level of the stories was equivalent to that of an American 6th grader (readability determined by a combination of tests including Flesch-Kincaid and Gunning-Fog, see (Jarrell, 2012).

The Mobile Learning Project

In 2009, the Mobile Learning Project (MLP) was begun at Shimane University. Unlike the Jaremaga Project, which has continued as a public email magazine, the MLP was restricted to students at one university. Participation in the Jaremaga Project was part of the coursework for the university students, but in the case of the MLP, participation was voluntary. Flyers were handed out to all first-year students who then registered their email addresses in order to take part in the project. Students who did not want to register their email addresses were still able to access the content on a blog site designed for both PCs and mobile phones. Up to February 25, 2015, this site got 117,984 hits from our students as well as hits from outside search engines. A total of 561 students, mostly freshmen when they joined, signed up.

The contents of the MLP were more varied than the Jaremaga

Project. Aside from the short English essays on different topics, similar to the essays in the Jaremaga Project, students were sent English grammar quizzes with Japanese explanations and TOEIC/TOEFL exam strategies, also in Japanese. Materials were sent out from one to three times a week as email texts with embedded links so that once the passage was read, the students could access a web page and leave comments or take quizzes. In this way, the MLP had a feedback loop that was lacking in the Jaremaga Project.

Reader involvement in content development: feasibility apparent from the Jaremaga example

While the Jaremaga Project did not offer a similar web-based feedback loop, some subscribers started to send essays directly to the author via an email address added to the email magazine in July 2008. The essays which were appropriate in terms of topic and length were edited and sent out as part of the email magazine. As the number of contributions grew, it became possible to set aside Friday as the "Readers' Corner" using only reader contributions.

As of May 2013, there were over 5,000 subscribers, and the "Readers' Corner" was in its third year. In that month, a questionnaire using google forms was sent out to the 61 readers who had contributed essays or long comments previously to investigate their motivation for writing. In the 24 responses, the reader-writers indicated that they were motivated by a need to communicate their own ideas, the desire to improve their English, and the satisfaction of seeing their work come out in the email magazine. One reader specifically mentioned enjoying reading the essays of other readers like herself. Reader contributions such as these indicated that reader involvement in content development was feasible.

2.3.3. Method

In the first stage of the new mobile learning project in 2013, students were hired as content developers and paid to develop English learning materials. This first stage, which finished in the spring of 2014, was followed by a second phase which calls for volunteers to contribute content. In this article we will report on the outcome of the first stage. Aside from the obvious difference of having student content developers, the 2013 project distinguished itself from its predecessors in its greater interactivity. There was also greater use of multimedia aids because reading accompanied by pictures and audio has been shown to be more effective than a text-only format.

Content development participants

Flyers were distributed to approximately 300 readers in June 2013 asking for participation as paid content creators. However, after one month, only five students had registered. As a result, in August, 2013, the authors started to verbally invite students who were thought to be interested in and capable of contributing to the project. By October 2013, a total of 22 students from the authors'

Chapter 2

two universities had joined the content development team.

These students were grouped into four content teams according to their preferences: the Essay Group, the Grammar/Vocabulary Quiz Group, the Joke, Riddle and Other Material Group, and the Technical Group. Of 22 student content developers, 17 chose to join the Essay Group to write essays. The participants ranged from first-year to fourth-year students from a number of different non-English majors in Shimane and English majors in Nagoya. All the student content developers were female with the exception of the technical team member, the only male participant.

Process of mobile learning content development

Induction began with an orientation explaining the purpose of the project, the ethics of e-learning material development and the types of content that were expected. The Essay Group was told that essays should be written in easy English and could be on any topic they liked or were good at. The essay length would be 80-140 words. Essay group members were asked to write carefully in English but not worry about perfection as the essays would be edited by a native English teacher before being sent out.

Their work was submitted through a Moodle forum which also allowed communication with teachers and other developers to be realized using Moodle messages and the Moodle plugin, Quick Mail. Teachers could access the students' work and edit it in the forum. All of the student writers were able to see each other's work and the edited changes. In the original MLP, jokes and riddles were reported to be the most popular teacher-created materials. Therefore, content in this project development included jokes and riddle writing, too.

Figure 1. Content submitted via Moodle forum

Figure 2. Student-developed mobile learning content – before and after teacher's editing

Chapter 2

Data connection and analysis

Students started to submit materials in October, 2013. Every contribution was carefully edited before it was sent out to subscribers. Teachers were responsible for ensuring error–free, natural-sounding English. Content originality and reusability in a mobile learning environment were also verified.

When the project ended in March 2014, we had received 52 contributions. The revised versions together with teachers' comments were available in the Moodle forum for all members to view. The forum was designed to allow student content developers to peer review or to engage in collaborative writing, although the only communications registered were between student and teacher. Data in three areas were collected:

1. Number of contributions and content features
2. Readers' attitudes and feedback toward student-developed content
3. Attitude and feedback of student content developers themselves

The Moodle system recorded the log-in history of every content developer. Readers' attitudes toward student-developed content were investigated in two ways: through a mobile web survey carried out in April 2014 with 12 questions asking about readers' general perceptions toward student-developed content and other aspects of the project, and by looking at the number of comments made by the readers on individual materials. We also investigated the attitudes of

71

the 22 content developers in March 2014 by sending them a separate survey asking about their thoughts on the involvement in the project.

In both surveys the system prevented duplicate responses. Students were encouraged to voice their real thinking about the project so they were not required to give their names.

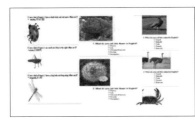

Figure 3. Student contributions
–vocabulary quizzes

Figure 4. Student-created
animation

2.3.4. Results

From October 1, 2013 to February 28, 2014, the project received a total of 52 mobile learning materials from the student content developers. Some students chose to ignore their original self-placement, and the majority of submissions (42) were essays, followed by essay animations (6), jokes (2) and quizzes (2). Of the 22 students who agreed to join the content development team initially, six never submitted anything by the end of the first stage. During the five months, four of the students submitted more than half the total materials, the most diligent contributor being a foreign student. Even when paid, most of the participants were not very active in content development.

Chapter 2

Table 1. Student-developed content - number of submissions in different categories

Content category	Essays	Jokes	Quizzes	Animations	Total
Number of submissions	42	2	2	6	52

Table 2. Number of submissions from individual content developers

Number of submissions	7	6	5	4	3	2	1	0
Number of content developers (Total: 22)	1	2	1	2	3	4	3	6

Readers' perceptions

We asked readers about their perceptions of student-created content through a survey in Japanese which was carried out from April 5 to April 30, 2014. The survey link was sent to the 344 subscribers at that time. Only 36 responded, a response rate of 10%, although the survey system did detect that many subscribers had opened the survey link and browsed the survey questions without answering the questionnaire. Of the total 12 questions, four directly concerned readers' attitudes towards student-created content. Question 1: What do you think of the idea of inviting students to write essays and quizzes? Question 2: How did you feel about student-developed learning content (edited by teachers) compared with teacher-created content? Question 3: Generally, how did you like the project after involving student content developers? Question 4:

What did you think of the length of the learning content sent out every week?

The results of readers' perceptions are shown as follows (n=36):

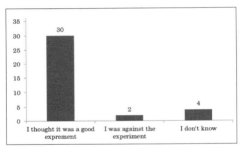

Figure 5. Readers' attitudes towards the idea of involving students (Survey Question 1)

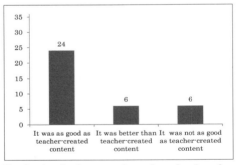

Figure 6. Readers' attitudes towards student-developed content (Survey Question 2)

Content developers' perceptions

Although the project received positive feedback from readers about student-developed mobile learning content, the voices of student content developers themselves needed to be heard. What motivated them to join the content development team? Since they were paid, was money a major consideration? We surveyed all the 16 content developers who had contributed content, nine of whom responded to the survey.

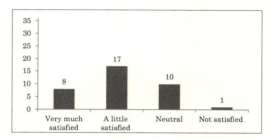

Figure 7. Readers' attitudes towards the overall project after involving students (Survey Question 3)

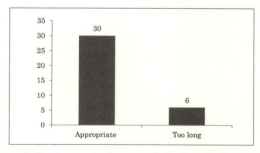

Figure 8. Readers' attitudes towards the length of materials (Survey Question 4)

Table 3. What content developers think about their involvement

1. What was the major reason for your participation in the content development team?

Reason	Good English practice	I was paid.	I learned from seeing the edited version.
Number of respondents	5	2	1

2. How much of the other students' content did you read in the submission system?

How much	All the submissions by others	Some submissions	None
Number of respondents	1	7	

3. Why did most of you choose to write essays rather than develop other learning contents?

Reason	Mobile learning essays are short and we are free to choose the topics. Essays are easy to write.	A native teachers carefully edits the essays.	Other
Number of respondents	6	3	1

4. In the content submissions, there was only two grammar quiz. Why were you reluctant to make grammar quizzes?

Reason	Don't know how to make a grammar quiz even with samples provided.	Hard to make an original grammar quiz.	Other
Number of respondents	1	5	1

5. In this project, you were requested to submit original content every 10 days. What did you think of the frequency?

Attitude toward the frequency	Just appropriate	Too frequent	Other
Number of respondents	5	1	1

6. What do you think of the level of the learning content developed by yourselves?

Attitude	Teacher-developed content is better	Student- developed content is better	Both are good
Number of respondents	5	2	1

Chapter 2

2.3.5. Successes

Data collected from both the content developers and the users has made it possible to judge the effectiveness of the project. Results of the data analysis highlight some aspects of the successes as well as the challenges of the project.

In terms of student-developed content, the readers seemed to have a favorable view of the project. 67% of the students surveyed stated that they enjoyed content created by peers and viewed those materials as equal in quality to those produced by teachers, although it must be acknowledged that the materials had been previously edited by teachers. There was no indication that students avoided student-developed content. In fact, 83% readers thought that student-created content was as good as that of the teachers, or even better. One reader commented: "It was stimulating to read our peers' essays or answer quizzes made by them." The same percentage of students (83%) thought that the length of content created by students was suitable for reading on mobile phones.

The majority of student content developers who responded to the survey indicated that their reason for joining the content development team was for the English practice. Indeed, when preparing learning materials, the students needed to do careful background research and try even harder than usual to write in "correct" English. Knowing that their contributions would be sent out to a large audience, they tended to prepare their materials more seriously. Their submissions were sent to a Moodle forum where they were accessible to the other content developers during their different stages of editing. It is unclear whether this kind of exposure at the beginning stage was beneficial or detrimental to their willingness to produce content. However, most of the student content developers reported reading the submissions made by the other developers with interest, reflecting the attraction of student-produced content.

The essays written by students were mostly about topics familiar to all the students: traveling, cultural differences, campus life and events they participated in. This kind of essay appears to strike a responsive chord in the hearts of their peers. As the materials are carefully edited by teachers, the accuracy of the English also allows the essays to be used as examples of good language usage in the mobile learning content database.

Even though students were paid for content development, the cost was still much lower than hiring teachers. The 52 submissions on different subjects from student content developers reflect what current Japanese students think, what they do and what they are interested in. Student-created content has enhanced the stock of learning content for this project and it may encourage other students to voluntarily contribute content.

2.3.6. Challenges

Certain problems became apparent as the project progressed. Paying students minimum wage did not motivate them to become active in the content development. As Table 2 indicates, of 22 registered content developers, six never contributed anything. These six students did access the submission system and read the guidelines and samples, but they chose to be silent. During five months of the project implementation, 10 content developers produced no more than three materials each. The most prolific writer, who wrote a total of seven essays, was an international student who was happy to receive payment for "studying."

The reason for the low output of many content developers may be due to a number of reasons. First, compared to a part-time job, the earnings from the project are irregular, so this kind of activity cannot take the place of part-time work. Another reason, as one student mentioned, is the difficulty of making original grammar quizzes. The process of writing essays may also be more difficult than the students had imagined. Several of the non-contributors mentioned a lack of time and ideas. This suggests that student content developers may need more support in their efforts, especially when all communication is done by email rather than face-to-face.

While it is true that teachers can save time by having students develop content, editing students' work and checking ethical issues can still be time-consuming. For example, a joke created by a student turned out to be copied from a web site. By the time the problem was discovered, the joke had already been sent to subscribers and added to the project database.

An interesting finding from this project is that readers and material developers had different perceptions of student-produced content. Whereas 83% of the readers considered student-created content as good as, or even better than teacher-produced content, more than half of the content developers thought that teacher-made content was better than theirs. This kind of perception may be a psychological hurdle preventing content creators from taking full advantage of this writing opportunity.

2.3.7. Conclusion

Based on the objective data collected from the project technical system and subjective perception feedback from readers and student content developers, the research questions have been answered: it is possible and feasible to have students develop mobile learning content. With teacher's guidance and supervisions, students have been shown capable of developing suitable mobile learning materials. Money is not the only incentive driving content development; more content developers in the project indicated that their motivation came from the opportunity to use English and have it corrected by a teacher. It is clear that only a few subscribers have a negative attitude toward learning content developed by learner themselves, perhaps due to student-created content being topical and campus life related. Further student-involved development of mobile learning materials may be more cost-effective than employing teachers to create them.

Despite these merits, there are many challenges: students in general lack enthusiasm in responding to call-for-content-development even when offered payment. The students involved in content development may actively make contributions in the beginning of the project, but with the passage of time, their contributions dwindle. Sustaining student content development remains a big challenge. Student-created content can provide a welcome infusion of creative and interesting materials to the mobile learning project, but most of the contributed content needs to be edited and revised by the teacher, sometimes with a substantial investment of time and energy.

Overall, in terms of involving students in mobile learning content development, we have discovered a number of successes, but the challenges to creating a sustainable project are equally daunting. It is hoped that building on these successes and overcoming these challenges may provide a way forward in content development activities in general e-learning.

(Section 2.3 was originally published in *Proceedings of ICHL 2015, Lecture Notes in Computer Science, Vol. 9167*, 382-393, with Douglas Jarrell and Jun Iwata.)

References

Cavus, N., & Ibrahim, D. (2009). Mobile learning: an experiment in using SMS to support learning new English language words. *British Journal of Educational Technology.* 40, 78–91

Chen, C-M., & Chung, C-J. (2008). Personalized mobile English vocabulary learning system based on item response theory and learning memory cycle. *Computers and Education*, 51, 624–645

Gümü, S.(2010). Rapid content production and delivery in e-learning environments: use of Adobe Presenter, MS PowerPoint, Adobe Connect. Procedia Social and Behavioral Sciences 9. 805–809.

Jarrell, D. (2012). Using a database of easy-to-read stories, *LET Chubu Journal*, 23, 11-18.

Levy, M. & Kennedy , D. (2005). Learning Italian via mobile SMS. In A. Kukulska-Hulme & J. Traxler (Eds.). Mobile learning: A handbook for educators and trainers (pp. 76-83). Taylor & Francis, London

Pinkman, K. (2005). Using blogs in the foreign language classroom: encouraging learner independence. *The JALT CALL Journal, 1(1)*, 12-14.

Pritchard, C (2008). Publishing L2 learner's writings on sites with user-generated content: analyzing the potential audience. The *JALT CALL Journal, 4(1)*, 30-39

Stockwell, G (2008). Investigating learner preparedness for and usage patterns of mobile learning. *ReCALL, 20(3)*, 253–270

Thornton, P., & Houser, C. (2002). Mobile learning: Learning in transit. In P. Lewis (Ed.), The changing face of CALL: A Japanese perspective (pp. 229–243). The Netherlands: Swets & Zeitlinger

Thornton, P., & Houser, C.: Using mobile phones in English education in Japan. *Journal of Computer Assisted Learning*, 21(3), 217–228 (2005)

Wang, S., & Smith, S. (2013). Reading and grammar learning

through mobile phones. *Language Learning & Technology, 17(3)*, 117–134 (2013) Retrieved from http://llt.msu.edu/issues/october2013/wangsmith.pdf April 25, 2019

2.4. Mobile Language Learning Styles of Japanese Students

2.4.1. Introduction

The rapid development of mobile technology is leading users from computer-based e-learning toward mobile phone-based mobile learning. Consciously or unconsciously, more and more people use mobile phones to learn, evidenced by the number of learning applications added either to Apple Store or Google Play Store every day. The mobile phone is no longer just a tool for conveying messages any more.

However, compared with PC-based e-learning, mobile learning does not enjoy the same level of maturity. Neither the technical systems nor learning content of many existing mobile learning projects ideally meet students' needs and expectations (Kozaki and Nishii, 2011). The mobile learning applications currently available for language learning serve as examples of such a misfit. Currently, most mobile assisted language learning applications focus on TOEIC/ TOEFL vocabulary, and the major type of interaction available for users is taking vocabulary quizzes. Reading, grammar, listening and speaking applications are not yet well developed. Many students start to learn on mobile phones with great enthusiasm but quit halfway. Furthermore, the majority of mobile learning applications are commercial in nature or linked to advertising. This could have a negative impact on the number of students willing to use mobile language programmes.

Chapter 2

In order to have students accept and welcome the concept of mobile learning, and accordingly enjoy the experience, teachers and mobile learning system designers should fully understand the mobile hardware readiness of students, their mobile learning styles, their preferences in study materials, and the optimal format of materials to be delivered, as well as their worries and concerns over carrying out mobile learning. For the purpose of addressing the above issues as regards Japanese university students, we analyzed the data collected from an ongoing mobile assisted language learning project being carried out at Shimane University, Japan, called the Mobile English Learning Project. With the support of the project data, this paper tries to answer the following questions:

1. Is the hardware environment suitable for Japanese university students to carry out learning via their mobile phones?

2. What kind of English learning content is suitable for students to study on mobile phones?

3. While teacher-created materials are currently dominant in mobile learning, do students welcome materials created by their cohorts?

4. During what time period of the day are students mostly likely to conduct mobile learning?

5. Are there other ways to keep students motivated in a mobile learning project besides creating high-quality materials?

6. What are students' concerns over their personal information and data security when conducting mobile learning?

2.4.2. A mobile assisted language learning project

In 2009, a mobile learning project aimed at improving students' English reading and grammar ability, called the Mobile English Learning Project, was initiated at Shimane University, Japan. The project is ongoing, with a total of 476 new students joining the project in 2013 and 2014. Most of the participants were first-year students at the time they joined. Before the project began, flyers were handed out to every first-year student to encourage them to take part in the project by registering their e-mail addresses.

The project regularly sends out a variety of language materials such as short English essays on different topics, English grammar quizzes, and TOEIC/TOEFL exam strategies. The materials are sent two or three times a week as e-mail texts with attached URLs which students can click in order to leave comments or take quizzes. Students register with the project of their own volition, and they are able to quit at any time. There are no required tests during the project, its sole purpose being to provide a ubiquitous environment for students to read English and learn or review English grammar without the pressure that they often encounter in the classroom.

In terms of English essays, there is a rich variety of topics: culture differences, entertainment, science and engineering, politics, economics, travel and campus life. English jokes and riddles are also sent out from time to time. In terms of grammar, a difficult item is explained in an e-mail message sent out. Attached to the e-mail message is a web link to a five-question quiz designed to reinforce

Chapter 2

the grammar points (see Figure 1).

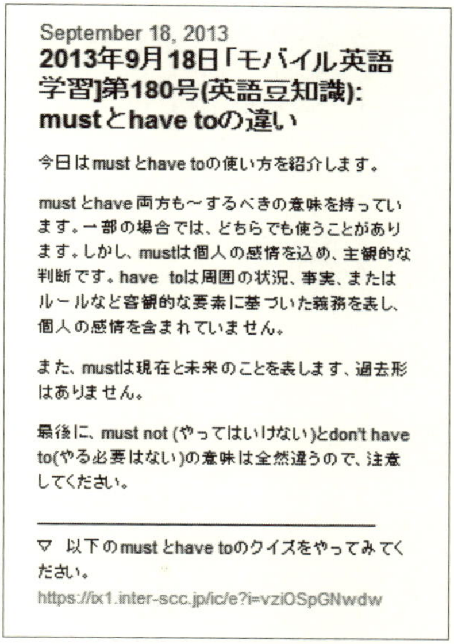

September 18, 2013
2013年9月18日「モバイル英語学習]第180号(英語豆知識):must と have to の違い

今日は must と have to の使い方を紹介します。

must と have 両方も〜するべきの意味を持っています。一部の場合では、どちらでも使うことがあります。しかし、must は個人の感情を込め、主観的な判断です。have to は周囲の状況、事実、またはルールなど客観的な要素に基づいた義務を表し、個人の感情を含まれていません。

また、must は現在と未来のことを表します、過去形はありません。

最後に、must not (やってはいけない)と don't have to(やる必要はない)の意味は全然違うので、注意してください。

▽　以下の must と have to のクイズをやってみてください。
https://ix1.inter-scc.jp/ic/e?i=vziOSpGNwdw

Figure 1. Grammar material sent by e-mail

Students who do not want to register their e-mail addresses but would like to read the content delivered by the project are able to choose to access a blog site designed for both PCs and mobile phones (Borau et al., 2009) (see Figure 2)

モバイル英語学習プロ
グラム
Learn English at anytime, anywhere!

March 1, 2014
2014年3月1日「モバイル英語学
習」第209号（エッセイ）: My
Sweet Memory

February 26, 2014
2014年2月26日「モバイル英語
学習」第208号（英語豆知識）:
An Animal Sound Quiz!

February 19, 2014
2014年2月19日「モバイル英語
学習」第207号（エッセイ）:
Movie Goers in Korea and the
U.S.

February 16, 2014
2014年2月16日「モバイル英語
学習」第206号（エッセイ）: The
First Day On The Job

next »

発信内容を検索!

[   ] SEARCH

최신 기사

テーマ

Figure 2. Essays archived in a blog site

In this project, each composition originally written by teachers is no more than 140 words in length so that it can be read in one or two minutes on a small screen (Grosseck and Holotesch, 2008). In order to appeal to a majority of first-year students, whose average knowledge of English is at a pre-intermediate level, all the materials are written in simple and easy-to-understand English. Any words that we thought might cause a problem are annotated with Japanese translations. Vocabulary notes are placed at the beginning of the essay to make readers aware of new vocabulary items before they read the essay (see Figure 3).

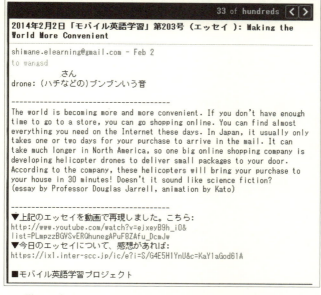

Figure 3. An essay example (see online version for colors)

There are a number of reasons for using in-house materials. Firstly, creating original reading and grammar materials avoids copyright issues. Japanese copyright law stipulates that a web page and all other related documents are copyright protected. Teachers may reproduce materials from web pages and use them in the classroom only if they do not 'unreasonably prejudice' the copyright owner. In essence, this implies that teachers must be careful to ensure that the only place they use the materials is in the classroom (Heffernan and Wang, 2008). Secondly, a teacher who is familiar with the students' learning needs is more likely to resonate positively with the students, enhance their classroomobile learning and, hopefully, increase their motivation towards language learning.

Also, from a teaching perspective, creating in-house materials enables teachers to offer material which learners themselves see as relevant and transferable to other situations. In order to appeal to our young cohort, the topics chosen for the mobile learning project are as topical and broad-based as possible. For the purpose of capturing students' interest, the chosen topics are not overly taxing and include jokes and riddles. Although listening skills have never been the main focus of this project, we were aware that reading accompanied by pictures and audio is considered to be more effective than text-only (Mansourzadeh, 2014). Therefore, some materials sent by the Mobile English Learning Project include both audio and visual content to support the readings.

2.4.3. Mobile learning features seen from Japanese project participants

On the registration page for the Mobile English Learning Project, students are asked about their reading devices, namely which mobile device they want to use to receive learning materials and

Chapter 2

whether they have a package payment plan giving them unlimited internet use. In addition, they are asked if they have previously used mobile devices for learning purposes. Every year, we also conduct online surveys in order to receive feedback from project participants.

The following data was obtained from 135 students registering in May and June 2014:

A: Which digital device will you use to receive learning materials?

• Smart phone – 83%

• Japanese style mobile phone – 4%

• PC – 12%

• Other (iPad, iPod, …, etc.) – 1%

B: Do you have an unlimited use package payment plan for the internet on your mobile phone?

• Yes – 83%

• No – 17%

C: Have you ever used mobile devices for learning purposes?

• Yes – 70%

• No – 30%.

The above data shows that the majority of these students possess multi-functional smart phones that are internet connected all the time. However, simple ownership of learning enabled devices does not guarantee that students will use mobile phones for learning. About 30% of the students claim that they have never conducted mobile learning before.

2.4.4. Students' preferences on mobile learning materials

During 2009 to 2012 in the Mobile English Learning Project, a total of 201 mobile learning materials were sent to student's e-mail addresses. Of them, 30 were on TOEIC grammar, vocabulary and strategies, 125 were English essays, 19 were about English learning methods, and 27 were grammar quizzes.

A survey is carried out every year to obtain subscribers' feedback about the learning materials sent out from the project. The survey conducted on April 2012 from the Mobile English Learning Project suggested that the idea of learning English on mobile phones and involving students themselves in creating mobile learning content is basically welcomed by the students.

Table 1 indicates that generally students accept the idea of learning on mobile phones and they consider reading materials and learning grammar on mobile phones to be helpful for improving their English ability. They prefer essays to grammar quizzes. Students like to read topics related to cultural differences, school life and entertainment. They are particularly keen on English jokes or humorous stories. Politics, science and technology are not popular with students, even though most of our readers, with the exception of a small group of medical students, are either social science majors or engineering majors.

The project has made the students realise that the mobile phone

Table 1. Students' preferences on mobile learning materials   Notes: Survey time: April, 2012. N = 56

Options	%	Responses	Options	%	Responses
1. Between November 2011 and March 2012, 30 topics were developed by students. What did you think of these materials?			*2. Overall, do you think that this project was helpful in improving your reading and grammar ability?*		
Good	64.30%	36	Very helpful	8.90%	5
Neutral	35.70%	20	Somewhat helpful	62.50%	35
Poor	0%	0	Neutral	25.00%	14
Other	0%	0	Not very helpful	1.80%	1
			Not helpful at all	1.80%	1
3. How often did you read the learning materials?			*4. Were the learning materials difficult?*		
All the	19.60%	11	Very difficult	3.60%	2
Sometimes	71.40%	40	Somewhat difficult	33.90%	19
Never	8.90%	5	Appropriate	62.50%	35
			Somewhat easy	3.60%	2
			Very difficult	1.80%	1
5. Which type of learning materials did you prefer?			*6. From the essays you read, what were your favorite topics?*		
Essays	41.10%	23	Environment	12.50%	7
Grammar	26.80%	15	Life/living/entertainment	26.80%	15
English	33.90%	19	Cultural differences	30.40%	17
All types	7.10%	4	English	12.50%	7
None	7.10%	4	English learning	5.40%	3
			Science and technology	3.60%	2
			Society	3.60%	2
			Politics	3.60%	2
			English jokes/riddles	44.70%	25

is not only a tool for voice communication, taking photos and gaming (Shibatari, 2010), but also a useful tool for learning English. One student interviewed said: "Before this project started, I used my mobile phone only for messaging, calling and playing games, or at best, as a built-in dictionary. Now I realize that a mobile phone can be used for learning!"

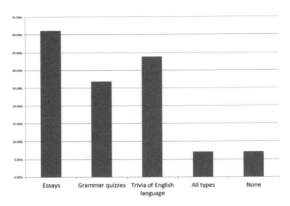

Figure 4. Students' ranking of favored learning materials
(see online version for colors)

According to the 56 responses, essays (41%) were the most popular, followed by trivia (34%), and grammar quizzes (27%). Further data analysis yielded more information on topic preference in essay writing and trivia. In order of preference, topics were ranked as follows: English jokes and riddles (45%), cultural differences (30%), life/living/entertainment (27%), and topics related to society (12.5%). Less popular topics included English learning methodology (5%), science and technology (4%), and politics (4%).

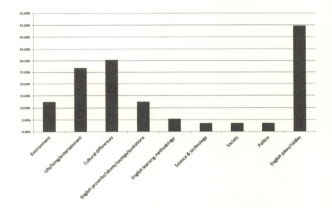

Figure 5. Students' ranking of favored essay topics
(see online version for colors)

The results imply that students prefer to read essays and trivia rather than to do grammar quizzes. Amongst all the topics, English jokes/riddles were ranked as the most popular, followed by cultural differences and topics connected to life/entertainment. The fact that essays are preferred to grammar quizzes should remind us that materials read or interacted with on mobile phones should not be overly demanding: students may not have the time or the energy nor do they have patience to do sustained study on small-screen mobile phones. Interesting materials such as English jokes and riddles, or something more esoteric, i.e., cultural differences or campus life, can better attract students' attention and provide stimulation for this kind of project.

2.4.5. Students' attitudes toward student-created mobile learning materials

In recent two decades, there is a trend toward student-led collaborative learning where teachers adopt a supportive role and become learning resources (Harden and Crosby, 2000). Students are entrusted with new roles as content producers. Mobile learning has certain characteristics that make it an attractive platform for materials development. First, the possession of mobile devices by all university students makes it possible for students to access materials at any time and place. The size constraints of the screens have led developers to create short, focused learning materials. Together, these characteristics make mobile learning a suitable area for research into the possibilities of student involvement in e-learning content development. Therefore, the Mobile English Learning Project invited more than 30 students to write essays and create other materials, and up to February 2014, the Mobile English Learning Project had received about 100 student-created materials. Student-created content need not be limited to written learning materials, but can also include multi-media materials. The follow is an animation developed by a first-year student at Shimane University.

Figure 6. Student-created animation – 'Make the world more convenient'

In the survey (see Table 1), the responses to Question 1 show that involving students in mobile learning material development was considered to be a success. 64% of the subscribers claimed they enjoyed the materials developed by their peers.

2.4.6. Student preferred mobile learning time

Table 2. Student mobile learning time

Time of a day	Number of submissions during the time	Percentage
Morning (5:01 ~12:00)	18	12%
Noon (12:01 13:30)	11	8%
Afternoon (13:31~17:00)	13	9%
Evening (17:01 ~20:00)	52	36%
Night (20:01~ 5:00)	52	36%

Cognizant of the fact that students can choose to conduct learning via their mobile phones at any time, we wanted to find out whether students had a preferred time of day for conducting mobile learning. The 2013 project registration page asked students what time of day they preferred to receive learning materials on their mobile phones. Students ($n = 137$) indicated their preferences as follows: anytime: 61%, evenings and night: 22%, lunch time: 14% and mornings: 3%.

In order to confirm that the above responses were indeed accurate, we randomly chose the access record data of seven quizzes and three essay comment interfaces which are kept on the server for objective investigation. Table 2 shows that 72% of quizzes and comment submissions occurred in the evenings and at night, followed in frequency by the mornings, the afternoons and noon.

2.4.7. Students' motivation of participating in mobile learning

In spite of some successes, the project has faced many challenges. The first challenge is the way to deliver the content. In total, up to September, 2014, the number of email addresses registered with the Mobile English Learning Project was 476. Unfortunately, not all of the registrants have become permanent participants; many subscribers' email addresses were found unreachable. The reasons ascribed to the loss of subscribers could be many (a) obviously, some students found that the project was not suitable for their learning style and chose to terminate their subscription; (b) Japanese students frequently change their mobile phone email addresses in order to avoid spam emails, but they forget to pass on this information to the project; (c) many students' mobile phones are pre-set by telecommunication companies to prevent receiving emails from PCs; and (d) they are too busy to do such an "extra" learning activity.

In addition, it is technically difficult to judge if a reader truly read the content or not unless he or she makes a comment or clicks the web link attached to the e-mail. The difficulty of tracking students' degree of involvement is the major hurdle we have faced so far. Of course, we can choose not to deliver mobile learning content via e-mail addresses but via web. The fact is, however, that content delivered via web may not have the same readership as e-mails. After all, students check e-mails very often, while they do not often come to a site. The solution to the dilemma of choosing a mode of delivering mobile learning content relies on students' learning motivation.

To keep readers motivated and responsive to mobile learning content is another great challenge. Although the survey indicated that students like topics in cultural differences and school life, the essays in these areas did not really have more responses than other topics did. In the project, messages receive an average of three rankings or comments while most readers remain silent. Even the English jokes that were perceived to be most popular with students had only five responses to each on average. Grammar and vocabulary quizzes never had good participation. The following figure shows that among 239 subscribers, 19 students took quizzes. This may suggest that no matter how well mobile learning content is designed, attaining a high degree of student involvement can be difficult if the task is voluntary.

Figure 7. Low participation (19/239) of vocabulary/grammar quizzes

(Section 2.4 was originally published in *International Journal of Innovation and Learning, Vol.19 (4)*, 431-443, with Douglas Jarrell and Jun Iwata.)

References

Borau, K.,Ullrich, C.,Feng, J.& Shen. R.(200 9). Microblogging for language learning: using Twitter to train communicative and cultural competence. *Lecture Notes in Computer Science, Vol. 5686, 78-87*.

Fiorea, S., Cuevasa, H., & Oserb, R. (2003). A picture is worth a thousand connections: the facilitative effects of diagrams on mental model development and task performance. *Computers in Human Behavior,* 19(2), 185–199.

Grosseck, G., & Holotesch, C. (2008). Can we use Twitter for educational activities? Paper presented at the Fourth *International Scientific Conference eLearning and Software for Education*, Bucharest, Romania.

Harden, R. M. & Crosby, J. R. (2000). The good teacher is more than a lecturer: the twelve roles of the teacher. *Medical Teacher*, *22*, 334–347.

Heffernan & Wang (2008) Copyright and Multimedia Classroom Material: A Study from Japan. *Computer Assisted Language Learning,* v21 n2 p167-180

Kozaki, Y., & Nishii, Y. (2011). All about smart phones (in Japanese). Nikkeibp: Tokyo

Mansourzadeh, N. (2014). A Comparative Study of Teaching Vocabulary through Pictures and Audio-visual Aids to Young Iranian EFL Learners. *Journal of Elementary Education Vol.24(1)*, 47-59.

Wang, S., & Smith, S. (2013). Reading and grammar learning through mobile phones. *Language Learning & Technology*, 17(3), 117–134. Retrieved from http://llt.msu.edu/issues/october2013/wangsmith.pdf

Shibatari, D. (2010). Surveys on trends of personal games. In: *Ketai White Book 2010*, 89–90. Impress R & D, Tokyo.

Chapter 3

Exploring Japanese Students' Mobile Language Learning Habits

3.1. Introduction

E-learning has witnessed explosive development in the last two decades. Cassette players, black and white TVs, and overhead projectors (OHP), which were common in foreign language classes in 1980s and 1990s, have almost disappeared. Correspondence-style courses relying on textbooks and radio or TV broadcasts have largely been replaced by digital materials. Multi-media learning materials such as audio, images, videos, and texts can now be easily transmitted via the Internet. Along with advances in hardware and networks, new e-learning software and systems have been developed.

Since the emergence of the iPhone in 2007, smartphones now have become the norm, with almost every learner possessing one. Accordingly, mobile learning has become an extremely important branch of e-learning. As Gros & Garcia-Peñalvo (2016) point out, "future e-learning should encompass the use of Internet technologies for both formal and informal learning by leveraging different services and applications."

Japan is a land of sophisticated information technology with one of the world's fastest mobile networks. E-learning is being carried

Chapter 3

out in all levels of schooling, especially in higher education. Many Japanese universities have integrated e-learning into their curricula. PowerPoint is no longer the only most common tool for "e-learning" as teachers move on to other forms of e-learning to assist their teaching, to assign and collect homework, and to contact students. Moodle, Quizlet, and podcasts are among the applications that are commonly used these days by language teachers. In addition, the Japanese government has set a goal of "one student, one tablet" for all schools by 2020 (Ministry of Education, Culture, Sports, Science and Technology – Japan (MEXT), 2015), thereby enhancing the e-learning hardware environment. Furthermore, active learning, an educational mode that involves students in the learning process more directly, is strongly supported by MEXT. According to Chen, et al. (2010), students with e-learning experiences have been shown to perform better in active and collaborative learning than students with only traditional class-learning. E-learning students are also more likely to use deep approaches of learning such as higher-order thinking and reflective learning

General "learning habits" refer to modes used by learners to process, organize and interact with learning materials (Kolb, 1984; Sadler-Simit, 1996). Gregorc (1985) asserted that almost 95% of individual learners have specific learning habits. In terms of e-learning, habits are the students' common styles of online behaviours. There are numerous e-learning research articles and reports available online or offprint, but most of the research focuses on specific e-learning systems and individual implementation of e-learning projects. Very few have discussed autonomous learners' learning styles, their habits and the evolution of these styles and habits over time.

Saeed et al. (2009) did discuss students' learning habits and their technology preferences, but their research was a case study focused on students' learning habits with blogs, podcasts and social book-marks, not with an entire e-learning course. Kim, et al (2011) compared SNS habits of Korean students and American students from a viewpoint of cultural differences. However, the SNS in this research was not for learning purposes. Chang, et al. (2009) developed a mechanism which can -identify students e-learning habits. However, the system was only tried out with elementary school students. Successful system application to university students has yet to be reported.

Among very few research papers discussing Japanese university students' e-learning and habits, Goda et al. (2013) categorized 7 types of e-learning behaviours after analysing data from a 15-week English course. As some "types" of e-learning behaviour were defined based on data from a very small number of students, they cannot be generalized for Japanese university students' e-learning habits.

Chapter 3

3.2. Research Purposes

In order to provide a general picture of Japanese students' e-learning habits, the authors started to collect relevant e-learning data eight years ago when they started integrating e-learning into the English syllabus. PC-based e-learning and mobile phone-based mobile learning were introduced to both regular courses and special English projects. Up to March 2018, 7535 students at the main campus of Shimane University had used an English e-learning program called Gyuto-e and about 850 students had used another e-learning program called ALC NetAcademy2. The MLP (Mobile Learning Project), a MEXT grant-supported mobile English learning project, was carried out at both Shimane University and Nagoya Women's University with an approximate total of 700 students registering from 2013 through May 2018. Students' learning data in these three projects has been carefully collected and stored on server. As the administrators of three different e-learning programs (see Figure 1,2 &3), the authors are authorised to access all logs and other learning records on the server systems where the above three projects reside. Besides, the authors conduct surveys every year to ask students to self-report their e-learning activities and perceptions.

Figure 1. Gyuto-e System

Figure 2. ALC NetAcademy 2

Chapter 3

Figure 3. Mobile Learning Project (Smartphone APP)

By analysing the objective server data and subjective self-report data that the authors accumulated from e-learning projects over the past years (2010-2018), this research aims to clarify the following behaviours and look into trends and changes.

1. What digital devices do students use to complete e-learning tasks? Computers or smartphones?
2. When students have a deadline, when do they actually complete an e-learning task?
3. Do students these days have more pre-university e-learning experiences than students in the past?

3.3. Method

Shimane University is a national university in western Japan. Every year about 1000 new students are enrolled to six different faculties of this university. As a part of general education, all of the first-year students are required to take an e-learning blended TOEIC-oriented course, with the exception of medical students. It is mandatory for students to complete online assignments every week on an LMS (Learning Management System). Students' learning achievements are measured using eight online quizzes and two summary tests. The data we focus on include students' login and logout time, time length of online participation, answer accuracy, and the system functions which are frequently used.

Gyuto-e is an online English learning program developed by an IT company in Hiroshima, Japan. The program itself is a user-friendly LMS with a database of 40 reading passages, 800 listening questions and 740 grammar questions. All of the questions are multiple choice. After the answer is submitted, students can choose to view audio scripts, re-listen to the audio, and read the detailed explanations if it is a grammar question. On the administration side, the teacher can view a variety of students' learning data and manage the learning process.

Gyuto-e has been integrated into a mandatory course for first-year students from five different faculties at Shimane University since 2010. Eight years of student learning data, including online test results, are stored on the server.

Chapter 3

Gyuto-e is basically a PC -based English learning program, although it is compatible with most smartphones.

ALC Net Academy 2, developed by Hitachi Solutions Ltd., is another English e-learning program used at Shimane University. Students at this university use various courses such as life sciences, medicine, and TOEIC preparation provided by the program. Students' learning outcomes are checked with multiple choice and fill-in-the-blank questions. As with Gyuto-e, students' learning performances are recorded in the system, and teachers can view overall class data or look into an individual student's learning history.

The Mobile English Learning Project (MLP) is a mobile language learning project jointly implemented by Shimane University and Nagoya Women's University. The project began in 2011 and sends various types of English learning materials to students' mobile phones twice a week. These materials mainly consist of short news and cultural reports, personal anecdotes, TOEIC study materials, and general knowledge quizzes. After students read the materials, they can choose to respond by taking short comprehension quizzes or giving feedback on what they read.

In terms of the first two English language e-learning systems, we look at concentrated login time, total online learning time and accuracy of the answers.

The MLP server also records students' access time and answer accuracy. When the students are asked to register with this project, they report their expectations about, perceptions of and preferences

109

concerning mobile language learning. In order to collect reliable data in different years, the survey questions have remained almost identical. In the registration form, we include the following questions.

1. Does your mobile phone contract have an unlimited data plan?
2. What kind of device will you use to receive mobile English learning content?
3. Have you ever used a mobile phone for learning before?
4. At what time of day do you prefer to receive English learning materials on your mobile phone?

3.4. Data Results

The Mobile Learning Project (MLP) was set up as a collaborative mobile learning project between Shimane University and Nagoya Women's University. Every year, we ask students to voluntarily register with the project so that they can receive English learning materials on their mobile phones. The registration page is in fact a questionnaire to determine their e-learning habits.

Chapter 3

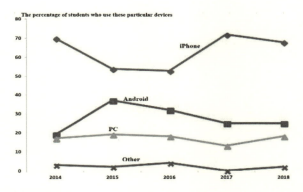

Figure 4. Most-frequently used device for receiving mobile learning materials

Note: The question "On which device are you going to receive mobile learning materials" was added to the registration in 2014.

This graph (see Figure 4) shows that in the two universities, the iPhone is the still most common device for mobile learning, with 53-72% of the total survey participants relying on it. 19-35% of students use Android smartphones. Just under 20% of students prefer not to use mobile devices and opt for the PC to receive small chunks of learning materials.

The following Figure 5 clearly shows that unlike 5 years ago, Japanese students now tend to use a limited data plan for their smartphones. Unlimited plan usage was 88% in 2013 but has declined to 39% in 2018.

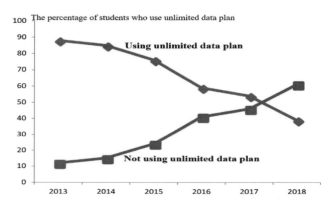

Figure 5. Use of mobile phone unlimited data plan

"When is your preferred time to receive learning materials on your mobile devices/PCs?" We have asked the same question to the Mobile Learning Project registrants every year since 2013. The students who answered this question changed every year, but the preferred time for receiving e-learning materials has shown little change (see Figure 6): evening and night remain the most favored times, while morning is ranked second. The afternoon is ranked as the least desirable time to receive learning materials on their mobile phone, which is consistent with the university students' schedule. They are unlikely to have time for learning online in the afternoon due to their university courses.

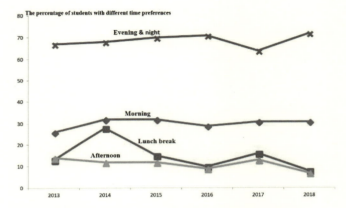

Figure 6. Most-favored time to receive learning materials

The data in Figure 6 only goes back to 2015, which was the first year students were asked if they had any experience using a mobile phone for learning prior to entering university. The number of students who have used a mobile phone for learning is gradually increasing. In 2018, 87% of first-year registrants reported that they had used mobile phones for learning before entering university.

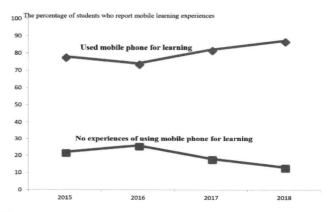

Figure 7. Pre-university experience using a mobile phone for learning

To conclude our findings from six years of data from registrations for a mobile learning project, the following two learning habits have remained unchanged. Evening and night are still the preferred mobile learning times, and the iPhone remains the most commonly used tool for mobile learning.

However, we have also noticed some changes in students' mobile learning styles: The number of students who use an unlimited data plan is decreasing, and more students enter university with prior mobile-learning experiences.

The above is the self-report data from students who participated in MLP projects in different years from 2013 to 2018. The following is the object server data from two syllabus integrated e-learning programs at Shimane University from 2010-2017: Gyuto-e and ALC NetAcademy 2

Chapter 3

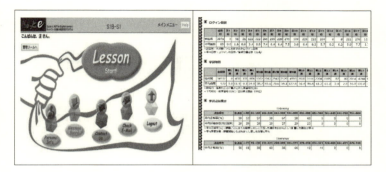

Figure 8. Syllabus integrated e-learning program - Gyuto-e

Figure 8 are screenshots of Gyuto-e. This e-learning program has been integrated into regular mandatory English courses in Shimane University since 2010. Although we encourage students to complete their online task using PCs, the system is also accessible via smartphones. Students are required to complete online assignments in this program, and teachers are provided with very detailed student learning data such as logins, learning hours, and answer accuracy by the system.

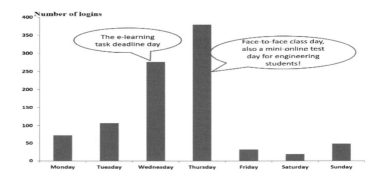

Figure 9. When students go online for their e-learning tasks
(n=36, 2017/10/4 - 2018/2/10, 15 weeks)

Note: Every Thursday was the e-learning class day when the teacher would talk about students' "online completion".

Figure 9 shows Gyuto-e login data of one 2017 class taught by the first author. There were 36 students in this class. They needed to complete 40 listening questions and about 30-40 grammar questions every week by 5 p.m. the day before their face-to-face class.

By analyzing the class login data stored on the server, we can see that most students only study intensively online the day before class day, which is the deadline for the online assignment. It is natural that that the largest number of accesses is on Thursday when students are required to take an online test in the Thursday face-to-face class. The second highest number of accesses is on Wednesday, the deadline for the assignment It is clear that when given an e-learning task and a deadline, students tend to go online right before the deadline.

Chapter 3

Students rush before the deadline, and they relax after the deadline passes. The two days after the class are when we record the fewest accesses. Interestingly, we found that on Sundays more students go online than Saturdays. This may be because the weekend is coming to an end, and students are starting to think about the coming week.

メール		学籍番号 🔼🔽	氏名 🔼🔽	クラス 🔼🔽	前回学習日 🔼🔽	学習回数 🔼🔽	学習終了ユニット数 🔽	進捗率 (%) 🔼🔽	サブコース合計学習時間 🔼🔽
☐	個人	1:		L1B-A2	2018/01/23	66	22	55	29:38:33
☐	個人	1:		L1B-A2	2018/01/24	76	22	55	12:01:45
☐	個人	1:		L1B-A2	2017/12/21	25	16	40	7:55:31
☐	個人	1:		L1B-A2	2018/01/23	43	22	55	21:07:33
☐	個人	1:		L1B-A2	2018/01/24	43	22	55	15:30:59
☐	個人	1:		L1B-A2	2018/01/18	70	20	50	12:27:23
☐	個人	1:		L1B-A2	2018/01/18	54	22	55	18:24:23
☐	個人	1:		L1B-A2	2018/02/01	67	22	55	21:01:06
☐	個人	1:		L1B-A2	2018/01/24	60	22	55	9:35:56
☐	個人	1:		L1B-A2	2018/01/23	74	22	55	23:14:02
☐	個人	1:		L1B-A2	2018/01/18	28	16	40	5:25:54
☐	個人	1:		L1B-A2	2018/01/23	43	22	55	18:09:14
☐	個人	11:		L1B-A2	2018/02/01	77	22	55	15:00:51
☐	個人	11:		L1B-A2	2018/01/18	40	20	50	17:38:53
☐	個人	11:		L1B-A2	2018/01/24	46	22	55	18:07:14
☐	個人	11:		L1B-A2	2018/01/24	102	22	55	31:55:50

Figure 10. Learning record of syllabus-integrated e-learning program - ALC Academy 2

Figure 10 is an online TOEIC course in the ALC Academy 2 program. We looked at average total online learning time and total logins per student in this e-learning integrated course. Students were required to compete 22 units in a TOEIC course in 15 weeks. We collected data from classes in the same course taught by the same teacher with the same syllabus to same level of students between 2014 - 2017. Here are the results (see Figure 11).

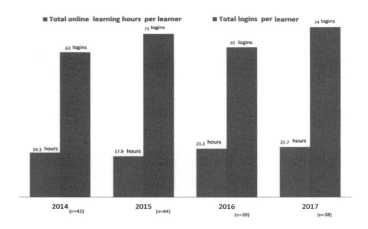

Figure 11. Total logins and total learning time for an online TOEIC course over four years

We didn't find any major changes in terms of total learning time and total logins in the past four years. This indicates that students' e-learning efforts for same e-learning tasks have remained unchanged over the past few years.

Chapter 3

3.5. Discussion

In this section, the authors will discuss the possible reasons for the observed e-learning habits and changes, and how online learning can be made more effective by taking these habits and changes into account. The iPhone is used more widely in Japan than in any other country in the world. Compared to a 20.32% overall share in the world market, the iPhone has a 66.5% share in Japan, while the Android only has a 32.57% share (AERAdot, 2017). Our surveys to the students in two universities confirmed this: 72% of MLP project registrants in 2017 and 68% in 2018 reported that they have iPhones.

This difference should remind e-learning teachers in Japan that when designing mobile language learning apps, the apps must be usable on iPhones. If the budget is too small to support the development of two different kinds of OS, one for the iPhone and one for Android phones, then iPhone app development should be given priority.

At first mobile data was expensive and Wi-Fi was not widely available, so students were concerned about the cost of their mobile data. They tried to avoid receiving any large audio or video files on their mobile phones. By 2013, 88% had decided to contract for an unlimited data plan which enabled them use as much data as they wanted. However, the portion of students who had unlimited data plans kept decreasing every year. In 2018, only 39% students signed such a plan with a mobile network provider. This may be due to the fact that Wi-Fi now covers most areas of the Shimane University

119

campus and students' apartments, so students no longer need unlimited mobile data from providers, or they just need a limited amount of mobile data when they are away from Wi-Fi. What is more, Wi-Fi is usually much faster and much more stable than mobile data. With these results in mind, e-learning system designers no longer need to be cautious about using videos and pictures. They can now develop materials without concerns about the students' ability to access these materials.

As to the appropriate time to be sent e-learning materials, the majority of students responded that evening and night are the preferred times. From this, it can be inferred that this is the preferred time for students to study. A plausible explanation for this preference may be that, in most cases, Japanese universities students have no classes at night. They have more time at their disposal and can learn online at their own pace. On the other hand, the afternoon is ranked as the least desirable time to receive e-learning materials, and hence the time of day when students are least likely to do e-learning. This is likely due to their schedule: they are occupied with classes or part-time work in the afternoon.

The increase in the number of students who had pre-university e-learning experiences is no doubt the result of guidelines set out by MEXT. MEXT has very detailed guidelines for information education in elementary and high schools (MEXT, 2008). Students are supposed to have basic IT skills before they are enrolled in a university. In addition, 86.1% of senior high school students are reported

Chapter 3

to have smartphones, and more than 83% access the Internet through smartphones rather than by PC. (Benesse Educational Research and Development Institute, 2014). Since the number of educational smartphone apps is increasing, it is quite understandable that more and more students have mobile learning experiences before they enter university.

Study habits with an integrated e-learning syllabus show certain clear tendencies. Students recognize that, as a part of the course, their online learning performance will be evaluated. They view every e-learning task as a type of homework and go online on the day of the deadline to get the tasks done. This is in spite of the fact that in the first author's blended learning class, students were repeatedly told to avoid procrastination and last-minute e-learning. Procrastination and deadline rush have existed every year in every blended class. This phenomenon has been noted in the research of Xu (2015) and Goda et al (2013). Actually, students may benefit from such procrastination in the post mini-test as they study right before the test day. However, in the long run, deadline rush negatively affects the learning outcomes (Milgram & Tenne, 2000). Indeed, in the authors' classes, students who always complete e-learning tasks well before the deadline had better scores on both mini-tests and final exams.

Once students complete their online homework and take the online post-test, they seem reluctant to study online again until they feel the new deadline approaching. This explains why in both

121

e-learning programs being used at the first author's university, the number of accesses is lowest on the day after the face-to-face class and then gradually rises as the deadline approaches. Teachers should be aware of such e-learning habits. In spite of the deadline rush tendency of most university students, we still need to set a deadline for every e-learning task. Otherwise students may not learn at all. Grit and self-discipline together with admonitions by their teachers may only work for a small group of very high motivated students (Wang & Smith, 2013).

It has been reported that that the time spent on task and frequency of participation are key factors for successful e-learning (Morris, Finnegan & Wu, 2005). However, over the past 4 years, no changes were observed in students' online participation. In a designated e-learning course, the average students' total online learning time and total login frequencies remained essentially the same from 2014 to 2017. There has not be a change in the behavior of students enrolled in recent years; they do not demonstrate any more diligence than their seniors in terms of e-learning, so teachers have no reason to increase the quantity and difficulty of assigned e-learning tasks.

3.6. Conclusion

By analyzing the long-term and follow-up data collected from two PC-based e-learning projects and one mobile phone-based e-learning project, the authors have found that in Japanese universities, there are twice as many iPhones users as Android users.

Chapter 3

Evening and night are perceived to be the optimal time for mobile learning, and perhaps for PC-based e-learning as well. When given a mandatory learning task, students tend to study most intensively right before the deadline. The cost of mobile data is no longer a big concern for mobile learning users due to the expanding availability of Wi-Fi and lower mobile data prices. More students had learning experiences with mobile phones before entering university. For a syllabus integrated e-learning program, no changes were witnessed in terms of students' e-learning diligence

The findings obtained from the two Japanese universities may be applicable to other universities in Japan. Some of e-learning habits of Japanese students may also exist in students of other countries. It is clear that when e-learning is employed, learners' learning devices, learners' learning styles, their preferred learning time and other learning habits should be taken into consideration. Fully understanding students' e-learning habits should help e-learning teachers design an appropriate and effective e-learning program. These findings, although drawn from language e-learning courses, may provide clues for e-learning in other educational areas as well.

The above findings describing common e-learning styles and habits of Japanese university students will be also useful in developing personalized e-learning systems using design system algorithms (Klašnja-Milićević et,al. 2011; Wang & Wu, 2011). This is another contribution that this research can make to the e-learning field.

(This chapter was originally published in *JALTCALL Journal, Vol.*

14 (3), 211–223, with Jun Iwata and Douglas Jarrell.)

References

AERAdot (2017). Why iPhone share in Japan is higher than it is in U.S. Retrieved from https://diamond.jp/articles/-/144140 on July 22, 2018.

Benesse Educational Research and Development Institute (2014). Survey of ICT Use in Japanese High Schools. Retrieved from https://berd.benesse.jp/up_images/research/ict_2014-all.pdf on July 25, 2018.

Chang, Y., Kao, W., Chu, C., Chiu, C. (2009). A learning style classification mechanism for e-learning. *Computers & Education*, *53*(2), 273-285.

Chen, D., Lambert, A. & Guidry. K. (2010). Engaging online learners: The impact of Web-based learning technology on college student engagement. *Computers & Education*, *54*(4), 1222-1232.

Dyer, J. & Osborne, E. (1996). Effects of teaching approach on achievement, retention, and problem-solving ability of Illinois agricultural education students with varying learning styles. *Journal of Agricultural Education, 37* (3), 43-51.

Goda, Y., Yamada, M., Matsuda, T., Kato, H. Saito, H. & Miyagawa, H. (2013). Categorization of Learning Behaviour in e-Learning. *Proceedings of 29th Annual Conference of Japan Society of Educational Technology.* 867-868.

Gros, B. & García-Peñalvo, F.J. (2016) Future Trends in the Design

Strategies and Technological Affordances of E-Learning. In Spector M., Lockee B., Childress M. (Eds) *Learning, Design, and Technology.* Springer, Cham, Switzerland.

Gregorc, A. F. (1985). Inside styles: Beyond the basics. Columbia, CT: Gregorc Associates.

Kim, Y., Sohn, D., Choia. S. (2011). Cultural difference in motivations for using social network sites: A comparative study of American and Korean college students. *Computers in Human Behaviour, 27* (1), 365-372.

Klašnja-Milićević, A., Vesin, B., Ivanovic, M. & Budiamac, Z. (2011). E-Learning personalization based on hybrid recommendation strategy and learning style identification. *Computers & Education, 56* (3), 885-899.

Kolb D. (1984). *Experiential Learning: Experience as the Source of Learning and Development.* Englewood Cliffs, New Jersey: Prentice Hall

Milgram, N. & Tenne, R. (2000). Personality correlates of decisional and task avoidant procrastination. *Personality, 14*(2). 141-156.

Ministry of Education, Culture, Sports, Science and Technology - Japan (MEXT) (2015). MEXT White Book 2015. p 384. Retrieved from http://www.mext.go.jp/b_menu/hakusho/html/ hpab201601/1375335_017.pdf on July 25,2018.

Ministry of Education, Culture, Sports, Science and Technology - Japan (MEXT) (2008). Digitization of Education Guide Book., Chapter4. Retrieved from http://www.mext.go.jp/b_menu/shingi/

chousa/shotou/056/gijigaiyou/attach/1259389.htm on July 22, 2018

Morris, L., Finnegan, C. & Wu. S. (2005). Tracking student behaviour, persistence, and achievement in online courses. *The Internet and Higher Education*, *8*(3), 221-231.

Saeed, N., Yang, Y., & Sinnappan, S.(2009). Emerging Web Technologies in Higher Education: A Case of Incorporating Blogs, Podcasts and Social Bookmarks in a Web Programming Course based on Students' Learning Styles and Technology Preferences. *Educational Technology & Society*, *12*(4), 98-109.

Salter, D. W., Evans, N. J. & Fomey, D. S. (2006). A longitudinal study of learning style preferences on the Myers-Briggs Type Indicator and Learning Style Inventory. *Journal of College Student Development*, *47*(2), 173-184.

Wang, S & Smith, S. (2013). Reading and Grammar Learning Through Mobile Phones. *Language Learning and Technology*, *17*(3). 117-134.

Wang, S. & Wu, C. (2011). Application of context-aware and personalized recommendation to implement an adaptive ubiquitous learning system. *Expert Systems with Applications, 38* (9). 10831-10838.

Xu, Z. (2015). Just Do It! Reducing Academic Procrastination of Secondary Students. *Journal of Intervention in School and Clinic*. https://doi.org/10.1177/1053451215589178

Chapter 4

Security, Privacy and Copyright Issues of Mobile Language Learning

4.1. Security

Japanese students are wary of clicking on any URLs that they are unfamiliar with. They fear that clicking on an unknown URL could result in spam email in the future or lead them to an untrustworthy website. In the interview with a student, we asked her concerns about receiving the learning materials on mobile. She reported: Clicking an unfamiliar URL sometimes directs one to a bad site. Not only does it cause spam emails, but also there is a high risk of being connected to potentially improper sites. So most of us are very wary about clicking on any suspicious looking links.

Indeed, in Japan, Internet fraud cases are becoming a major problem, as there have been cases whereby people have unknowingly clicked on a suspicious web link at work or in the public domain, with embarrassing consequences. In computer literacy courses high school and university students are repeatedly told not to click on any URLs that they are unsure of as computer viruses and personal information leaks may follow. For such reasons, concerns about security are regarded as a significant reason for low participation in some mobile language learning projects.

4.2. Online Privacy: Perceptions of Students

4.2.1. Introduction

Mobile language learning research has witnessed a great development in recent years. Numerous publications are now available academically. However, most of such research papers focus on technology, strategies and students' learning gains. Very little research looks at the issues of how online privacy discourse affects students' online-learning motivation. In this section, the author will address the following issues:

1. How much are East Asian students concerned about their e-learning privacy and what types of e-learning private information are they concerned about most?

2. What are students' perceptions toward online private information collection and monitoring by their teachers for learning purposes?

3. Do students in different countries have different perceptions on their online private information and are these perceptions changing over time?

4.2.2. Method

Participants

For the purpose of verifying if students' perceptions of e-learning privacy vary over time and country regions, surveys were carried out in two East Asian countries: Japan and China - during April 2009, and July 2012. Totally 800 students took part in the surveys. All

Chapter 4

participants were familiar with studying in one or more e-learning environments. There is no big gap in participants' ages.

Table 1. Participants of e-learning privacy survey

Survey year	Country	Number of participants of participants			Average age	Surveyed universities
		Male	Female	Total		
2009	Japan	151	104	255	19.1 (SD=2.7)	Hiroshima Shudo University, Yamaguchi University
2009	China	83	224	307	21.3 (SD=3.3)	Yangzhou University, Shandong University of Chinese Traditional Medicine, The Open University of Nantong City, Ningbo University of Technology, Jiangnan University
2012	Japan	120	55	175	20.2 (SD=0.8)	Shimane University
2012	China	43	20	63	20.7 (SD=2.12)	Anhui Jianzhu University

Aside from the above questionnaire, the investigation on user registration information from Moodle – a popular open-source LMS and another e-learning program called InterCussion was conducted in 2013 by one of the authors in Japan. Profiles of 152 users on Moodle and 109 registers on InterCussion were examined.

Data collection

The survey conducted in 2009 were in paper-and-pencil format. The printed questionnaire was distributed in class by the teachers and collected in class when it was answered. Completed question-naire sheets collected from 5 different universities in China were

129

posted to Japan for manual transcribing. The survey in 2012 was carried out online. Students were asked to access the survey URL and finish the questionnaire online. On Japan side, students filled in the questionnaire in PC classrooms with their teacher in class. On China side, the survey URL was sent to 78 students by email. And 63 students responded within a one week duration. As the survey was answered at ones' own volition for Chinese students, it was designed to refuse repeated submission from the same IP address.

When survey data was gathered and analyzed, one author in Japan accessed Moodle and InterCussion as a system administrator role to analyze real registered users' profile information.

4.2.3. Results

Survey Results

The questionnaire consisted of 8 questions and a request to give one free comment (See Appendix). The first question gathered demographic data such as the participants' gender, age and grade level. Questions 2-8 elicited participants' perceptions and attitudes to e-learning privacy disclosure. These questions (2-8) can be grouped into the following three categories:

(1) Questions investigating participants' self-assessment of their knowledge of privacy protection laws (Question: 2)

(2) Questions investigating participant attitudes toward the current use of their private information by their teachers (Questions: 3, 6, & 7).

Chapter 4

(3) Questions investigating the degree of participants' concerns over specific items of private information (Questions: 4, 5, 8).

Most of countries in the world have promulgated laws to protect people's privacy (OCED,2006). However, in different countries, people's understanding and recognition of the laws may be different. Question 2 asks students in Japan and China to self-rank their knowledge toward privacy protection laws. See Fig.1 below.

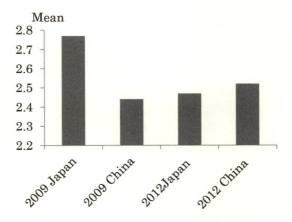

Figure 1. Students' self-assessment on privacy protection law knowledge
(5: Very familiar; 1: Don't know at all)

The data shows that students in both countries are aware of the existence of privacy protection laws, but are not very confident with their knowledge on the laws.

In 2009, Japanese students self-ranked higher than Chinese students, and in 2012, the result reversed. However, both differences are not statistically significant according to *t*-test (t(560)=1.423, p<.05, t(368)=0.190, p<.05).

Students' attitude toward teachers' collection of their online registration information as well as learning information are the very factors that this study tries to delineate. If students are too much fearful of their online private information being stolen, leaked or sold to a third party they will not be willing to join any e-learning program or actively involve in any online-learning activities. Therefore, it is not overstating to say that online privacy issues are one of the keys for a successful e-learning project (Jerman-Blaz̆ic̆ & Klobuc̆ar, 2005). The data in terms of students' attitude towards email address collection, online-learning monitoring, as well as their concerns of private data leakage are shown as follows.

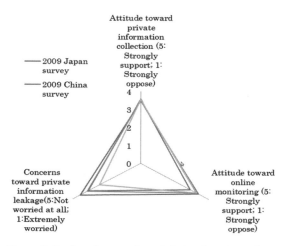

Figure 2. Students' perception of their e-learning privacy

The graph clearly shows that in general students in both countries support their teachers' collection of their email addresses, and understand and trust their teachers' monitoring their learning history and learning preferences on e-learning systems. However, degrees of support and understanding are different. Japanese students are more supportive of letting their teachers use their private data while Chinese students are more cautious. (Online monitoring: t(560)=5.54, p<.05; Concerns of private data leakage: t(560)=5.88, p<.05). Statistically, there is no difference between the attitude of Chinese students and Japanese students toward email address collection by their teachers. Difference between data in 2009 and 2012 is not significant, either.

Question 4 asked about what communication tool, PC email or mobile phone email/Short Message Service (SMS), that students preferred to use for contacting and being conducted in terms of e-learning matters. The result shows in the following graph.

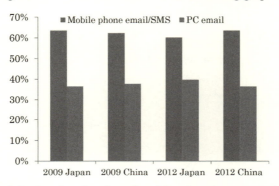

Figure 3. Students' preferred email tool for e-learning communication

The data implies that majority students both in Japan and China preferred to use mobile phone for message communication in e-learning. And these preferences did not change with passing time.

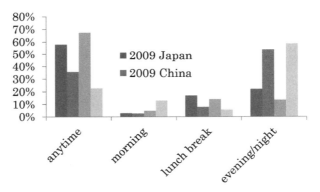

Figure 4. Student preferred time to be contacted

Question 5 investigated students' preferred time for being contacted via mobile phone. The data shows more than half of Japanese students (58% in 2009 and 67% in 2012) think they can be contacted at any time. Chinese students (54% in 2009 and 58% in 2012) preferred evenings or night for e-learning contact. A very small percentage of Chinese students regard lunch time as a good time for contact. See Figure 4.

The purpose of Question 8 is to find out when students register with an e-learning system what type of private information they are most reluctant to share. The results show that regardless of regions, 2012 or 2009, the private information that students are most reluctant to disclose is personal photos, mobile phone numbers, and physical address. The data further indicates that Japanese students (51% in 2009 and 45% in 2012) regard personal photo as the top sensitive information and they do not want to upload to e-learning systems. While Chinese students (35% in 2009 and 32% in 2012) think their mobile phone number is the private information that they are most cautious to disclose. The other sensitive private information and less sensitive private information are also shown in Figure 5. There is no statistical significance between the student participants in the same country in 2009 and in 2012, which means no change over time can be seen in students' perception towards what is sensitive private information.

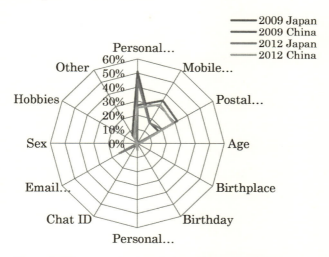

Figure 5. What type of private information are students most cautious about?

For most of survey items participants are encouraged to write down reasons for their answer. And the final item of the survey is to ask participants' general comments on e-learning privacy. These comments directly from learners provide the first hand source to expound the survey outcomes. The Discussion part will look closely into students' written feedback.

Registration Results in e-learning systems

Three of the above surveys were administered in classrooms with teachers in class. Students answered the questionnaires, either by paper- and- pencil or online, then turned them in to the teachers. The existence of teachers could give students a certain kind of pressure so that students may "positively" rank their attitude regarding survey items in which teachers seemed to be involved (Yoshimura, 2001). Thus, in order to confirm the results obtained in the subjective surveys, the objective registration data in e-learning systems is gathered. We first investigated students' registration information on an email magazine project performed in 2012 which aimed at improving students' English reading ability. Among the 109 students who registered at their own volition, 72 (66%) registered with their mobile phone email addresses, and only 32 (34%) registered with their PC email address. This result conformed with what was discovered in previous surveys: mobile phone email address is preferred for e-learning contact.

Moodle's "edit profile" module provides many fields for users to

Chapter 4

share their private information. See Figure 7 and Figure 8. One author investigated profiles of 152 registers as a Moodle administrator. He discovered that all of the students registered their real names, cities, countries. Regarding email addresses, as they were told that Moodle is mainly a PC-oriented LMS, all of them registered with PC email addresses. Nobody uploaded their personal photos or registered any other private information.

Figure 6. Moodle user profile page (1)

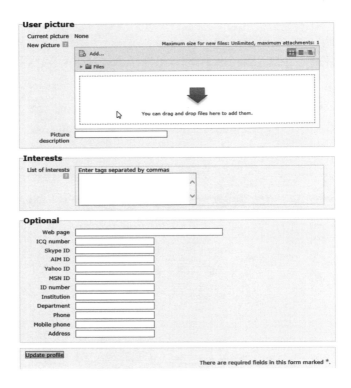

Figure 7. Moodle user profile page (2)

4.2.4. Discussion

Personal information/privacy protection is an ongoing concern in our information society. The majority of countries in the world have drafted laws to protect its peoples' personal information/privacy from intrusion (OECD Report, 2006). In e-learning, learner concerns over the security of their personal information/privacy heavily influence a learner's willingness to disclose information on themselves in online activities. The more learners are concerned about the security of their online private information, the less they will disclose about themselves (Dinev,Hart & Mullen, 2008). Teachers cannot force or pressure students to provide personal information even for learning purposes. However, when an e-learning teacher better knows the personal information/privacy concerns of their students, they will be better able to decide what information to collect and how it should be used. Teachers can feel more secure collecting information that students are willing to divulge than information learners are hesitant to disseminate. Not only should teachers be familiar with personal information protection laws, they should also ask what concerns their learners have about e-learning privacy and personal data disclosure.

In Japan the Act on the Protection of Personal Information (Cabinet Office Government of Japan, 2005) is strictly enforced and widely publicized by mass media. In China there has not been a special private protection law so far, however, privacy protection is formulated within other laws, such as the China Civil Law. In recent years, China has witnessed a breath-taking development in Internet use and now has the most Internet users in the world (CNNIC, 2013). Online privacy has become a daily topic for ordinary Chinese people. Further, in both countries, cyber-crimes are often reported in the news. This makes online privacy concern deeply-rooted among the citizens. However, being aware of the existence of privacy laws does not mean students have read and understand details of the laws or use the laws to protect their cyber interest. This may explain why students in both countries did not rank their knowledge of the law very highly.

Since university students claim to have some degree of knowledge of privacy laws, e-learning teachers too should undoubtedly also read concerning private information/privacy law provisions, and/or attend their institution's training seminars regarding the laws, in order to be equipped with enough legal knowledge to address issues of private data disclosure in e-learning.

Email is still the most commonly used private information for exchanging e-learning content (Levy & Stockwell, 2006). Thus collecting email addresses is very common in an e-learning class. In some e-learning systems, like Moodle, email based registration is a must. The surveys we carried out in Japan and China show that learners in both countries, to a large degree, support email address collection and see it as a necessary, or at least as a "have-to" requirement. For the sake of convenience, the majority of young students prefer to use mobile phone to receive messages from teachers. This is because mobile phone is a carry-on tool and can deal with any urgent task anytime, anywhere. In Japan, almost all mobile phones are internet-connected and every mobile has a unique email address. In China, mobile phone email is not recommended by telecommunication contractors, but SMS is always available at good service. As smart phone has now rapidly become the norm for a progression of

Chapter 4

university students, Yahoo email, Gmail and Hotmail - which were regarded as PC email accounts - are now also checkable at fingertip. Nevertheless, one Japanese survey participant commented:

> For class announcement or short, text e-learning materials, I would like to receive on mobile phones, but for a big chunk of materials, please send to my PC email address.

This comment reminds teachers of the fact that the mobile phone is an ideal tool for message communication, but not good for heavy e-learning tasks.

Besides positive attitude toward email collection, students in both countries also understand teachers' online monitoring on their learning progress. One Chinese participant commented:

> I don't feel comfortable when I realize that my leaning is being watched by teachers. However, without "spying" on us, our teacher would not know how well or how poorly we are doing online. Monitoring or even tracing our learning history is acceptable to me as it is for learning purpose.

Students are cautious about their online private information, but are not worried about their private data being leaked to a third party. Two students' comments may backup this confidence:

> I am not worried at all about our private information stored in e-learning systems. First of all, I trust our teachers can safely handle our private information in a secure way. Second, if by any chance, the system is hacked, who want to buy our learning information? Our credit number is not there! (20 year-old first year Chinese boy

141

student)

I think the security of our e-learning system is tight. And I don't think our teachers will neither "sell" nor "tell" our private information to other people. It is not worth anything. (19 year-old first year Japanese girl student)

Interestingly, either in 2009 or 2012, Chinese students were found to be less forgiving than Japanese students in terms of online monitoring and online-learning security. The reason for this might be due to the factor that in China e-learning is mainly used for degree education (Kang & Song,2007) and is not integrated to general high education as widely as in Japan. And Internet security is not receiving the same attention as in Japan. Five Chinese students commented in 2009 survey that they have experienced email virus or fraud calls to their mobile phones.

Chinese students and Japanese students differ in preferred time being contacted via mobile phone. Most Chinese students take a nap at noon. Therefore the lunch break is not considered to be a good time for any learning task. They feel relaxed and have most free time in the evening or at night. Evenings or night is the best time to contact student's' mobile phone. While for Japanese students, most of them do not sleep at noon and they tend to place their mobile phones on manner mode whenever they are busy. This explains why the majority of Japanese students think they can be contacted "anytime".

Neither Japanese nor Chinese university students consider age,

Chapter 4

personal URLs, birthplace, chat-ID (Instant Messenger ID), and email address to be very sensitive; whereas they are very concerned about uploading their personal photos, telephone numbers and physical addresses. The top sensitive private information for Japanese students is personal photos while Chinese students regard mobile phone numbers as the most sensitive. The reason for this difference remains unclear to the authors and needs to be probed from cultural, social and economic points of view.

Students can control the content of their blogs and home pages. Similarly their chat-ID and e-mails can contain as much, or as little, self-revealing content as the student wishes (for example, you can give yourself any "name" you wish in your e-mail). However, students cannot control the information contained in their facial photos, home addresses or telephone numbers (Boston, 2009). One obvious recommendation therefore is that e-learning teachers in Japan and China avoid collecting or encouraging registration of students' facial photos, telephone numbers, and postal addresses. Regardless of the type of private information being collected from students, e-learning teachers should always make clear the reasons they collect private information from students, and always allow the students to refuse. When using private information, teachers must notify the learners. If personal student information is to be provided to a third party: for example, to another e-learning teacher - this requires consent from the individual student/s. Finally, when learners request modification of their personal information, the request has to be met (Japan Personal Information Act, Chapter 4, Article 18).

4.2.5. Conclusion

Perceptive data from the surveys coupled with objective data from actual in-use e-learning systems is carefully analyzed in this study. The findings show that learners in both China and Japan have positive attitudes toward private/personal data collection by their teachers if for learning purposes, although they did express concerns about some particular privacy items, such as personal photos, postal addresses and phone numbers. Japanese students are the most cautious with uploading of personal photos, while Chinese students are most reluctant to give out their mobile phone numbers. When having options, students in both countries choose to use mobile phones for message communication unless the message contains a large size of attachment. Although learning messages can be sent to Japanese students' mobile phones at any time; for Chinese students, evenings or night is the most ideal time for them to read and respond. Lunch time is fine for Japanese students, but should be avoided for Chinese students, as most Chinese take a nap after lunch.

There is no statistical significance found to imply that students in the same country perceive e-learning privacy differently from what they did three years previously.

By looking into the registration information in two e-learning systems, the above findings obtained from surveys were confirmed. E-learning privacy concerns prevent students from sharing any further information other than required items even with their teachers and cohorts.

The findings via this research indicate that teachers should collect as little personal information as possible. If really necessary, teachers should take into account that students are more concerned with some aspects of their privacy than others, and therefore teachers should do their best to find out which information their learners are apprehensive about providing. For the e-learning system designers, they should take the findings in this paper into account and design a system that is both effective and privacy risk-free.

4.2.6. Research limitations

While asserting East Asia, the surveys were only conducted in Japan and China. Certainly, Japan and China are important East Asian countries; however another advanced country in e-learning, Korea, is not concluded in this research. This could heavily lower the research reliability as a research from "East Asia". Further, on Japan side, this research only surveyed Japanese learners of English. On China side, this research mainly surveyed students majoring in English language or art. And analysis on actual e-learning registration was not performed in China as such an investigation needs a system administrator account. The results may display limitations unique to the region and foreign language learners; the same questions posed to learners in Korea and other academic disciplines might yield different responses.

References

Boston, J.(2009) Social Presence, Self-Presentation, and Privacy in Tele-Collaboration: What Information Are Students Willing to Share? *Journal of the Research Center for Educational Technology (RCET), 5(3)*. Retrieved April 30, 2013 from <http://rcetj.org/index.php/rcetj/article/view/64/128>

Cabinet Office Government of Japan (2005). Act on the Protection of Personal Information. Retrieved on April 29, 2013 from <http://www5.cao.go.jp/seikatsu/kojin/foreign/act.pdf>

CNNIC(2013).Statistical report on Internet development in China. Retrieved on April 30, 2013 from <http://www1.cnnic.cn/IDR/ReportDownloads/201302/P020130312536825920279.pdf>

Dinev, T., Hart, P., & Mullen, M. (2008). Internet privacy concerns and beliefs about government surveillance – An empirical investigation. *The Journal of strategic information and systems, 17(3)*, 214-233

Japan E-learning Consortium (2008). E-learning White Paper., pp. 58-64. Tokyo Denki University Press: Tokyo

Jerman-Blaz˘ic˘, T. Klobuc˘ar (2005). Privacy provision in e-learning standardized systems: status and improvements. *Computer Standards & Interfaces, 27*, 561–578

Kang, F., & Song, G.(2007). e-learning in Higher Education in China in Spencer –Oatey (Ed.) e-learning Initiatives in China. Hong Kong . p.31

Levy, M., & Stockwell, G (2006) CALL dimensions: Options and

Chapter 4

issues in computer assisted language-learning. N.J.: Lawrence Erlbaum Associates, Inc.

Li., X & Deng, S. (2010). Status Quo of E-learning Resources and Services in Project 211 Universities in China. *Journal of Library Research. Vol.12*. Retrieved August 7, 2013 from http://www.cssn.cn/67/6700/201209/t20120929_86160.shtml

OCED (2006). Organization for Economic Co-operation and Development: Report on the Cross-border Enforcement of Privacy Laws. Retrieved on April 30 ,2013 from <http:// www.oecd.org/dataoecd/17/43/37558845.pdf>

Yoshimura, T. (2001). Respondents' perspective and characteristics. *Journal of mathematical statistics 49(1)*, 223-229

Appendix: A Survey on personal data disclosure

1. Which year are you currently in?

    1) first year 2) second year 3) third year 4) fourth year

    5) fifth year 6) sixth year 7) graduate student

    Sex 1)male 2)female

    Age_____

2. Are you familiar with the Protection of Personal Information Act of Japan/ privacy protection laws in China?

               5   4   3   2   1

    <u>Very familia</u> ☐ ☐ ☐ ☐ ☐ <u>Don't know at all</u>

3. What is your attitude toward teachers asking for private information such as your e-mail address?

5   4   3   2   1

<u>Strongly support</u> ☐ ☐ ☐ ☐ ☐ <u>Strongly oppose</u>

Reason (   )

4. Do you prefer to be contacted through your mobile e-mail address/SMS or your PC e-mail address?

1) Mobile phone e-mail   2) PC e-mail   3) either one is fine

Reason (   )

5. Considering your own privacy, which part of the day do you prefer course-related material to be sent to your mobile phone?

1) morning   2) lunch break 3) evening /night 4) any time

Other time (   )

Reason (   )

6. In e-learning, some of your online activities, such as your login time-learning history, and learning preferences will be recorded and monitored. What do you think of this?

5   4   3   2   1

<u>Strongly support.</u> ☐ ☐ ☐ ☐ ☐ <u>Strongly oppose.</u>

Reason (   )

7. Are you worried that the personal data stored in your e-leaning

Chapter 4

program will be stolen or passed on to a third party by your
teacher?

5   4   3   2   1

Not worried at all ☐   ☐   ☐   ☐   ☐ Extremely worried

8. When you register your personal information with an e-learning
    program, which of the following personal items are you most
    reluctant to release?
    1) e-mail address 2) mobile phone number 3) birthplace
    4) age 5) address 6) photo 7) personal homepage/ blog site
    8) chat ID (Instant Messenger ID) 9) other (   )

9. Feel free to write down your comments on the issues regarding
    e-learning and personal data use and protection.

4.3. Copyright and Multimedia Classroom Material for Mobile Language Learning: A Study from Japan

4.3.1. Introduction

The section outlines the knowledge and attitudes that 57 language teachers in Japan have regarding copyright laws in relation to using external materials in language classrooms. A 13-item online survey was distributed, and semi-structured interviews were conducted, to ascertain what teachers know about Japanese copyright laws, and the teachers' resultant attitudes and actions regarding these laws. After introducing the theoretical background to the problem, this section delineates how the survey was carried out and then presents the data obtained. By examining themes culled from the survey and the interviews, three distinct categories were found: participants' knowledge about copyright laws; participants' intentions and actions in using external materials; and participants' attitudes toward copyright laws. The results indicate that while most teachers are aware of the existence of copyright laws, they do not act in a manner that suggests they are particularly concerned about them. That is, teachers in Japan use copyrighted material because it suits their lesson planning, and do not always consider the consequences of their actions. Further, the researchers demonstrate that teachers view copyright laws as being too vague and strict, ultimately affecting teachers' actions when producing and using materials. The study reveals the need for educational institutions in Japan to take the appropriate steps in providing adequate copyright law training for their teachers.

Language teachers worldwide make daily decisions on materials for classroom use: what to use, how to use them, and the applicability of the material to the learners they have in mind. This paper is of specific relevance to teachers who use media to facilitate language teaching and learning in the classroom. With myriad other issues to consider when creating and using digital materials in the classroom, there are teachers who do not ponder whether these materials are legally available for use. While most teachers are aware of the existence of copyright laws, many are unsure of their exact nature and how they relate to the day-to-day management of the classroom. This begs the question: is this acceptable behavior, or does there need to be a more earnest approach in addressing the issues that are encoded in the copyright laws of each country?

4.3.2. Research purposes

This study set out to investigate teachers' knowledge and attitudes toward copyright laws, and their behaviors and intentions in producing materials when they are unsure of the exact nature of such laws. Since the study was conducted with language teachers in Japan, the researchers endeavored to examine what knowledge these teachers have of copyright laws and to what extent do they go to investigate their responsibilities in regard to these laws? A further purpose of this study is to ascertain what teachers in Japan represent as being important when it comes to these laws. Mainly, how – if at all – do these laws affect teachers' selection of materials for the classroom and the resultant lessons planned around these materials? Do teachers deem it acceptable to use copyrighted materials in the classroom when the materials are being used for educational purposes?

Definition of terms. The term external materials will be used throughout this section to refer to all materials for classroom use that are produced by those other than the teachers using them. While some of the materials discussed in this section are copyrighted and some not, the main issues spring from the line drawn between the two. Furthermore, the types of materials discussed in this section include those that derive from the use of the Internet and computer-based multimedia that play audio and video material, display animation, graphics and text, and utilize the four macroskills of reading, writing, speaking and listening (Davies, 2007; Warschauer, 1996). This essentially entails any form of digital presentation, and presents a surfeit of benefits for teaching and learning in the second and foreign language (SL/FL) learning classroom. The term CALL practitioners refers to teachers who endeavor to use mixed media to enhance language learning and teaching, transforming both the content and processes of SL/FL education (Warschauer & Meskill, 2000).

Theoretical background In order to determine language teachers' knowledge and attitudes towards copyright laws, it is necessary to outline the copyright laws that currently exist. It is important to

Chapter 4

note that there has been surprisingly little research done in regard to CALL and copyright laws. However, there has been research conducted regarding copyright laws and how they effect education in general. Although this paper deals with the situation in Japan, it is often the case that teachers refer to, or have knowledge of, copyright laws in the United States (Karjala & Sugiyama, 1988), so some parallels can be drawn between the two countries. For example, both are signatories to the Berne Convention of 1899, and its successor, the Rome Convention of 1979 – the primary copyright conventions governing written and artistic material in the world today. Japan has consistently signed on to both, including the latest revisions in 1971 and 1989 (Copyright Research and Information Center, 2006a), and both give protection to material produced in either country. Thus, material produced in one country is protected in the other. With advances in technology come new concerns for MALL practitioners in the realm of the copyright laws that govern the use of classroom materials. Advances in communication and information technology have had a dramatic effect on copyright and intellectual property rights (Malonis, 2002; Miller, 2004). However, copyright laws tend to be quite Byzantine and most teachers do not pretend to understand their complexities.

While copyright laws may seem particularly strict, there are certain allowances for education, criticism, research, and scholarship (Malonis, 2002; Moore, 2005). Consequently, teachers engaged in such activities do have some leeway under the law. However, if teachers are to successfully integrate the materials they create and use in the classroom, they need to be aware that they can find themselves in a quandary if they do not have adequate knowledge of these laws. Hence, all language teachers need to keep abreast of how best to deal with the issues that affect them when choosing, creating, or copying materials for use in the classroom.

Japanese copyright laws. The laws governing copyright are written to ensure the rights of the copyright owner (Simons, 1995, p.80). In Japan, the following are prohibited: (1) copying whole versions of materials; (2) copying parts of materials that are limited in availability; (3) copying materials for marketable uses; and (4) copying large quantities of materials: the more copies that are made, the greater the infringement on the commercial rights of the owner (Copyright Research and Information Center, 2006a; Kato, 1994).

Essentially, this indicates that teachers are advised to be aware of the laws that exist before using any copyrighted materials in class, and to be conscious of whether or not they are breaching these rules. The basic premise of Japanese copyright laws center around what is considered a work. Japanese copyright law (Chapter 2, Section 1) stipulates that a webpage and all other digital media are considered works, and are thus protected by the copyright law (Copyright Information Center, 2006a). Article 35, Section 1, of the copyright law states that teachers may reproduce materials from webpages and use them in the classroom only if they do not 'unreasonably prejudice' the copyright owner (Copyright Research and

Information Center, 2006b). In essence, this implies that teachers must be careful to ensure that the only place they use the materials is in the classroom, and that the specific type and number of digital media made does not infringe upon the rights of the copyright owner. However, it is not clear as to what constitutes 'unreasonable prejudice' towards the original author (Simons, 1995). If teachers have an honest approach to using copyrighted materials in the classroom, they are on the right track. Namely, if they copy limited parts of digital media and use them for educational purposes, make only enough copies for classroom use, and do not intend to market said materials, they are within the bounds of Japanese law (Simons, 1995). Kato's (1994) criteria gives some insight into what this entails. However, in the case where ambiguity still exists, it is sensible for teachers to ask for permission to use the materials in question from the publisher or author (Copyright Research and Information Center, 2006a; Simons, 1995; Simpson, 2005). But how many is too many? The answer to this question is not so cut-and-dry. Often, a contract between teachers and publishers is drawn-up in order to specify exactly how many copies of the material (a computer program, material on the Internet, CD-ROM or DVD) are needed. Any amount of copies made over this number is a breach of copyright law (Copyright Research and Information Center, 2006b). Is it important to note that a web page need not have a copyright notice on it in order to be protected by the law (Crews, 2003; Horton, 2000), so MALL teachers should bear in mind the nature of the material they are downloading, and act accordingly. Finally, and perhaps most pertinently for teachers in Japan, Japanese law stipulates that educators are often permitted to make copies of computer programs or webpages for personal use. However, when this use turns into a public display of the material, copyright laws have been violated (Copyright Research and Information Center, 2006b). Therefore, teachers are advised to closely examine the section of the law that affects them the most.

The doctrine of fair use and digital media. The doctrine of 'fair use', which covers the rights of free speech and public interest in the United States (Malonis, 2002; Moore, 2005), is well known amongst educators. These laws are based on the existing laws in the United States (Copyright Law of the United States of America, 1976), and though there are no specific fair use laws in Japan, there are similarities in the manner in which Japanese law is interpreted (Karjala & Sugiyama, 1988). In fact, many teachers in Japan assume that the doctrine of fair use applies to the Japanese setting (Karjala & Sugiyama, 1988). Fair use allows teachers to copy small amounts of material for educational use. Horton (2000, {9) asserts that under fair use regulations, educators are permitted to use 1,000 words (or 10%) of a publication; 10% or 30 seconds of a piece of music; and the same amount of motion media. Furthermore, educators may not copy more than one complete work or two excerpts from the same author; copy from the same work more than three times; and copy from the same item more than once in an academic year. Lastly,

156

teachers must include the appropriate copyright information on all material they use in the classroom (Horton, 2000). Copyright protection encompasses much of the material used in educational programs. It manifests itself in nearly all original works by an author (Crews, 2003). In addition, most computer programs, writings and images are protected by copyright law (Crews, 2003, {4). Thus, when educators use any of these materials in their teaching, they are, in effect, using copyright-protected materials. Educators often use the doctrine of fair use to justify copying, scanning, downloading, uploading, and using materials for classroom use. While they often may be within the bounds of the fair use law, the fact remains that the exact parameters of the law are flexible and uncertain at best (Crews, 2003; Simons, 2005), meaning due diligence is required on the part of teachers when performing these acts.

Teachers' perceptions of copyright laws. The perception among teachers with knowledge of both the copyright law of the United States of America (1976) and Japanese copyright laws is that the definition of what is and is not copyrighted is confusing at best. Many teachers believe they can make copies of portions of materials (such as podcasts, recordings, or digitalized texts) for educational purposes (Coyle, 1996), and that materials on the web can be freely used in the classroom (Simonson, Smaldino, Albright, & Zvacek, 2003). This is, however, a misguided perception. In Japan, the mere act of downloading the contents of a webpage without authorization for use in a classroom is a violation of copyright law (Copyright

Research and Information Center, 2006a). In sum, when doubt exists about the nature of the law, it is best to investigate. The laws themselves are not easily understood, and cover unfamiliar ground for most language teachers. Therefore, researching the appropriate laws, or asking for permission from the author or publisher is a wise approach for teachers who are unaware of their rights.

4.3.3 Methods and techniques

Participants. A 13-item online survey (see Appendix) inquiring about teachers' knowledge and opinions of copyright laws in relation to language teaching was distributed to 80 university teachers working in different locations across Japan, the majority of whom are members of various well-known CALL organizations. The 80 teachers were contacted via email with a brief letter of explanation outlining the nature of the research. The method of sampling was purposeful sampling, as the researchers were interested in teachers who have an active interest in CALL and were using multimedia and the Internet to assist their teaching at the time of the survey in April, May and June of 2007. Fifty-seven teachers (n=57) – 43 native speakers of English and 14 native speakers of Japanese – responded with effective submissions (a response rate of 71%), and completed the survey within two weeks of receiving it. Participation in this research project was voluntary, and the participants were assured their answers would be anonymous.

Procedure. The survey had a combination of closed and open

-ended questions (Nunan, 1992) so that it would obtain as much tangible information as possible from the participants. The questions were designed to elicit the knowledge that teachers in Japan have of copyright laws, and how this knowledge affects their use of materials in the classroom. Before distributing the survey, a pilot study involving seven teachers was conducted, which resulted in the survey being adjusted in accordance with the seven participants' comments on some ambiguities in it (Wiersma, 1986). The individuals in the pilot study were not included in the actual study. The final question on the survey allowed for comments to begiven by participants. Many of the participants chose to avail of this option. In addition, semi-structured interviews were conducted with 10 of the participants (seven native speakers of English and three native speakers of Japanese) during May and June of 2007. This gave a qualitative aspect to the research and allowed the researchers to gain a deeper understanding of the teachers' knowledge and opinions of copyright laws in Japan. Coupled with the online survey, these served as the primary sources of data for this research project. Data from the survey were collected online with each answer automatically added to the database on authors' server. Each participant was permitted to submit the survey only once.

4.3.4. Results data analysis

After all the submissions had been received, the authors collected the raw data and analyzed it accordingly. The data distribution was tested by performing a t test in order to see if the results had statistical significance. The resultant significance level was 0.05. The quantitative and qualitative elements of the survey and the responses given in the interviews were analyzed for emergent themes (Cohen & Manion, 1994; Taylor & Bogdan, 1984). Three distinct themes were found: (1) participants' knowledge about copyright laws; (2) participants' intentions and actions in using copyrighted materials; (3) participants' attitudes toward copyright laws.

Participants' knowledge of copyright laws. The actual knowledge that the participants have of Japanese copyright laws is an essential component of this research. What the participants actually know of the laws determines their actions when it comes to selecting materials for their classes. As Table 1 demonstrates, over 40% of the participants have never read Japanese copyright laws. This is a rather large proportion, and when coupled with the 53% who have only limited information about the laws, a vast majority of participants in this study are represented. Moreover, most teachers (88%) have never attended training sessions on copyright laws. Both are significant numbers, as they allow us to see a larger picture of the knowledge teachers in Japan have of copyright laws and their significance for classroom practices. The responses to the survey also demonstrate that 77% of the participants believe that showing recorded programs from television and radio in class might conform with copyright laws, while only 22% of the participants realize that

Chapter 4

showing rented CDs and DVDs in class is an infringement of law. In accordance with these findings, the participants had a wide range of comments regarding their actual knowledge of Japanese copyright laws. The following comments were accrued from the surveys and during the interviews:

If I use a TV program or movie from a P2P (peer-to-peer) service, then it's a violation of the law. But if it's a news article, for example, then I think we're dealing with 'fair use'.

Table 1. Questions pertaining to participants' knowledge of copyright laws (n=57)

Question	Yes	No	Have limited information on the laws
2. Have you ever read Japanese copyright laws?	4 (7%)	23 (40%)	30 (53%)
Question	Yes	No	Not sure
3. Have you ever participated in copyright law training seminars?	7 (12%)	50 (88%)	N/A
5. Is it a violation of the law if you digitally reproduce commercial textbooks?	46 (81%)	2 (3%)	9 (15%)
8. Is it a violation of the law to show rented videos, DVDs or CDs in class? (*optional: n=36)	8 (22%)	11 (31%)	17 (47%)
10. Is it a violation of the law to show programs recorded from television or the radio?	13 (23%)	23 (40$)	21 (37%)

*Note: If participans answered 'no' to Question 7 on the survey, they did not have to answer question 8, so 36 responses were recorded.

A lot of sites I use indicate whether or not their material is reproducible or not; otherwise, I consider whether anything I'd like to copy is likely to be in the public domain.

I realized that I know very little about these laws. I would appreciate knowing the 'correct' answers to the questions on the survey.

161

The comments confirm the findings presented in Table 1. Specifically, many teachers are largely unaware of what Japanese copyright laws consist of, but do possess some concern over their liability when using materials in the classroom. One participant made the following comment:

The only knowledge I have is of the warnings that appear at the beginning of videos or when you first install software. I would like to know more in order to do what is right.

Those teachers who have knowledge of parts of the law seem to be unsure as to how far the law actually reaches:

It seems to me there might be question about 'commercial use' vs. 'private use' in some cases of copying and distributing copyrighted material in classrooms.

In my opinion, if the materials are used for educational purposes only, then copyright laws are not violated.

Thus, while some teachers possess a cursory knowledge of copyright laws – a knowledge that exists from reading some of the law or from seeing warnings and copyright symbols on documents – this knowledge is not enough to guide them in their day-to-day practices as language teachers. Most seem to feel that more guidance is warranted to allow them to gain the necessary knowledge about copyright laws.

Participants' intentions and actions in using external materials. The results of the survey indicate that the participants have a distinct impression of what they should do when uncertainty over the nature

Chapter 4

of copyright laws arises. In response to Question 6, 51% of the participants claimed that they judge materials to be copyrighted if they have a claim of 'Copyright Reserved' clearly marked on them, while 49% stated that everything on the Internet is copyrighted if original. Moreover, in response to Question 12, 56% of the participants stated that they make their own decision on whether or not to use materials when they are unsure of copyright laws, while 28% maintained that they actively investigate as to the legality of using external materials. Among the 36 participants who have showed rented CDs and DVDs in their classrooms, 8 (22%) claimed that they were aware their actions violated copyright laws, while 17 (47%) were unsure if their actions were an infringement of copyright laws. This indicates that even though some teachers are aware that their actions are an infringement of the law, they do not let this stop them from using such materials. Figure 1 demonstrates teachers' intentions and actions towards creating their own materials and using external materials. Some of the participants' comments regarding their intentions and actions towards using external materials expressed these feelings:

I assume everything is likely copyrighted. However, the chances of getting caught if you are not selling the materials you use for teaching is quite low. Essentially I, and I believe many other teachers, are unconcerned (about being caught) with burning CDs etc., for use in the classroom.

The materials should be marked in some manner. I believe there is

163

ample material that is considered a part of the public domain.

Some of the participants stated that their knowledge of the law affected their intentions and actions when using materials in the classroom:

It depends on where you get the materials. It also depends on how you use the materials.

I try to live up to 'fair use' as I understand it.

I have searched for the laws in the past. They are quite confusing, so I gave up.

However, some participants clearly know they are breaking copyright laws but carry on using copyrighted material anyway:

I try to use common sense. It is recognized as OK to use published materials without written consent, like when developing entrance exams.

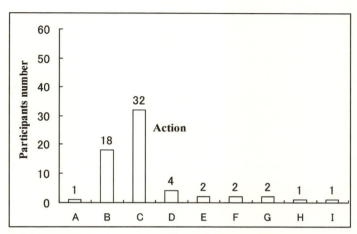

Figure 1. When producing or using materials for teaching and are unsure whether you are contravening copyright laws, what do you usually do?

Note: Some participants gave more than one answer to each question.

A-Ask lawyers or copyright law professionals

B-Investigate on the Internet or in the library

C-Make own decision according to my existing knowledge of the law

D-Decide against producing materials

E-Ask colleagues or consult language laboratory staff

F-Ask publisher of the materials

G-Do it anyway

H-Make sure the materials are on school server with firewall

I-Use materials discreetly

> Basically, I just do it. I use what I need, when I need it.
>
> I use materials anyway. I don't worry about it.

These last set of comments suggest that teachers either guess at what is right or break the law intentionally. While this latter group may be in the minority, there needs to be a better way of disseminating information about copyright laws to teachers so that they are aware of the consequences of their actions. Teachers' actions towards copyright laws are a direct representation of how they view the law and whether they see it as being important or not. These decisions hinge on whether teachers have the requisite information regarding the laws. Precariously, a majority of teachers (56% of the participants in the survey) make their own decisions about whether or not to use external materials – whether they are found on the Internet or come from other multimedia sources – when they lack enough knowledge of copyright laws. Even though 32% of the respondents maintained they actively investigate as to the legality of using copyrighted materials, this number does not indicate how far teachers actually pursue the issue and how it affects their lesson planning.

Participants' attitudes toward copyright laws

Another component of the research was to investigate participants' feelings towards violating copyright laws. Question 11 on the survey assessed the degree of fear teachers have of violating copyright laws. The results (on a four-point scale: 4 – very fearful to 1 – not at all fearful) delineate how fearful teachers feel about breaking copyright laws. Table 2 represents these feelings. From Table 2 it can be established that Japanese teachers have a much higher degree of fear of violating copyright laws (Mean ¼ 3.214, SD ¼ 0.579)

Chapter 4

than native English speakers (Mean = 2.233, SD=0.895). This correlates to the higher percentage of Japanese participants who have read or partially read copyright laws (64%) than the native speakers of English who have done so (56%) ($t(55) = 3.84$, $p<0.05$, unpaired t-test). Correspondingly, reading copyright laws seems to have an effect on teachers' attitudes and feelings towards the laws. The participants in the study have clear attitudes towards copyright laws. These ranged from not heeding the laws at all to worrying about the laws while keeping their learners first and foremost in their minds. The next comment reflects this last view:

My first concern is for developing my students' ability. At the moment I think copyright laws are too difficult to manage. I have in the past requested the right to use something but have not received a reply. I think the law has to be much more simple and much better disseminated.

One participant demonstrated knowledge of parts of the law and claimed this knowledge affected his/her teaching practices:

It may in fact be against the letter of the law, but not the intent, so I think it is alright to use the material in question.

167

Table 2. Participants' feelings towards unintentionally violating copyright laws when creating materials for classroom use.

	Degree of fear of Japanese participants (n=43)	*Degree of fear of native English speakingparticipants (n=14)*
Mean	3.214	2.233
SD	0.579	0.895

Finally, some participants strongly felt that universities had to put strict guidelines in place in order better police copyright infringements. The following participants acknowledged the lack of knowledge among teachers when it comes to copyright laws, and felt that university administrators should do more to inform teachers of their responsibilities:

I feel that fixed guidelines tailored to university workers are strongly necessary.

Although it is ultimately my responsibility to be aware of these issues, school administrations should also have some hand in ensuring their instructors adhere to the laws.

In the digital age, all teachers should really know more.

These days, copyright issues are getting more serious in university; for instance, making entrance examination questions which sometimes cite existing materials. We need to be better informed of the law in order to proceed correctly when making materials.

Therefore, the intent of most teachers is not to blatantly break the law. In fact, it can be ascertained that while not all teachers in this study think about the consequences of their actions, there is a general desire for more information regarding their responsibilities when it comes to copyright laws.

4.3.5. Discussion and conclusion

Language teachers may make honest efforts to avoid violating copyright laws, but there are bound to be those who do it unintentionally anyway. However, as with most aspects of law, ignorance is no excuse. Actively investigating the copyright laws of the country in which we live and practice our profession will assist in finding out what is legally required of us. While it may be inherently difficult to prosecute copyright violators (especially small-scale infractions) from any country (Simpson, 2005), educators have a moral and ethical responsibility to ponder the materials they use in the classroom (Malonis, 2002; Witherspoon, n.d.) and the consequences of using these materials. Language teachers regularly use external materials in their classes, whether they are from the Internet, CD-ROMs, DVDs, or peer-to-peer services. With regard to copyright laws, the results of this study demonstrate that teachers regularly make their own decisions on how to use materials in the classroom. Many participants revealed that they do not give a second thought about using the Internet or multimedia in the classroom. These conscious decisions either break the laws, or abide by them. Some participants in the study commented that they use common sense when making judgments regarding materials use. While this shows that teachers actively think of what is right and wrong, it does not solve the problem of using copyrighted materials without permission. Moreover, teachers in this study claimed to know they were violating the law when using these materials, but continued to use them anyway. These teachers asserted that as long as they were using the material for educational purposes, then it was acceptable behavior. Clearly, this is not the case and there needs to be a more transparent way of dealing with the issue.

Another salient element of the research is the feelings of Japanese teachers towards violating copyright laws in comparison to the feelings of native English speakers. Namely, the Japanese teachers are much more afraid of contravening the law than their native speaker counterparts. Thus, there is a clear need to have more of the latter group read the laws than is currently occurring. Whether this would have the desired effect or not (native English speakers being more aware of their moral, ethical and legal responsibilities) remains to be seen. This is an area that needs to be investigated further.

4.3.6. Proposed solutions

In light of this research, the authors can suggest some solutions that will assist in furthering understanding on the significant issues raised in the paper. These include, but are certainly not limited to:

(1) Teachers ought not to take copyright laws for granted. Using external materials for 'educational purposes' does not keep teachers safe from copyright infringements, and using 'common sense' does

Chapter 4

not always make clear sense in the eyes of the law. These teachers should take the time to read copyright laws carefully, especially those that deal with digital media use in the language classroom.

(2) The findings of this study correlate with Bamford's (1988) assertion that due to a lack of knowledge of copyright laws teachers often must make their own judgments as to whether they are breaching these laws. Consequently, universities ought to give clear guidelines on copyright laws so that teachers know exactly what they can and cannot do. Teachers should endeavor to obtain the necessary information from university administrations, academic conferences, and training seminars. As suggested by numerous teachers in the interviews, information needs to be disseminated to them via university administrations. However, teachers must also share the burden of investigating their responsibilities. Thus, by thoroughly investigating the issue, teachers can enlighten themselves as to what effect copyright laws have on their teaching.

(3) Teachers should be prepared to develop more of their own original materials. As time consuming as this may be, it is the best way to safeguard themselves from unnecessary legal trouble. One advantage of this approach is the familiarity we gain with materials we have had a hand in producing, thus allowing us to provide more effective lessons for our learners.

(4) Teachers should work closely with legal authorities in order to loosen the restrictions of copyright laws. In a world where the Internet has made geographic borders almost non-existent, those

wanting to see a freer use of resources can work towards these ends. Although this may not be a realizable goal in many parts of the world, at the very least it will intensify awareness about the nature of copyright laws among teachers and the need to work within the bounds set out by them.

Furthermore, as found in this study, many teachers are aware of some aspects of the law. However, the vagueness of the laws negatively affect teachers' motivation to abide by them when developing and using external materials for classroom use. If the laws continue to be vague and incompatible with teachers' practices, e-learning and copyright laws will continue to be uncomfortable bedfellows, which may negatively impact the development of the field of MALL itself.

This study was conducted in Japan, and the results may only pertain specifically to Japan. However, the results should make CALL and MALL professionals in other countries carefully consider their own responsibilities in terms of the laws where they reside. Namely, CALL and MALL practitioners can use the results of this study to examine their own knowledge, intentions and attitudes about the copyright laws in their countries and how they affect their classroom practices. The results of this study are conclusive, and a nexus exists between the actions of teachers with regards to copyright laws and the moral and ethical accountability of teachers in Japan. Education and information hold the key here: spreading the word on copyright laws and how they affect language teaching can

Chapter 4

greatly assist in preventing infractions of the law. The issues raised in this paper are relevant to all language teachers: they affect us all and we need to be aware of our responsibilities under the law.

Teachers should ask themselves how often they actively think about the issues raised in this study and how their decisions with respect to copyright laws affect their teaching practices. Language teachers, materials developers and administrators must genuinely assess the consequences of their actions, and if these result in both compliance with the law and adherence to the high professional standards that is required of us to provide our learners with quality lessons in the classroom.

(Section 4.3 was originally published in *the Journal of Computer Assisted Language Learning, Vol.21 (2)*, 167-180, with Neil Heffernan.)

References

Bamford, J. (1998). Setting up a library of English language movies. The Language Teacher. Retrieved June 2, 2007, from http://www.jaltpublications.org/tlt/files/98/aug/bamford.html.

Berne Convention for the protection of literary and artistic works (Paris Revision, 1971), Article

Cohen, L., & Manion, L. (1994). Research methods in education (4th ed.). London: Routledge.

Copyright Law of the United States of America (1976). Title 17 of the United States Code, Public Law 94-553, 90 tat.2451 (revised to February, 1993). Retrieved May 15, 2007, from http://www. copyright.gov/title17/.

Copyright Research and Information Center (2006a). History of copyright systems in Japan. Retrieved May 30, 2007, from http://www.cric.or.jp/cric_e/csj/csj.html.

Copyright Research and Information Center (2006b). Copyright case study Vol. 1: Formal education and copyright. Retrieved May 13, 2007, from http://www.cric.or.jp/cric_e/cs_1/case1.html.

Coyle, K. (1996). Copyright in the digital age. Retrieved June 6, 2007, from http://www.kcoyle.net/sfpltalk.html.

Crews, K. (2003). New copyright law for distance education: The meaning and importance of the TEACH Act. The Copyright Management Center. Retrieved June 15, 2007, from http://www. copyright.iupui.edu.

Davies, G. (2007). Introduction to multimedia CALL. Module 2.2. In G. Davies (Ed.), Information and communications technology for language teachers (ICT4LT). Slough: Thames Valley University. Retrieved October 15, 2007, from http://www.ict4lt. org/en/en_mod2-2.htm.

Horton, S. (2000). Simplified fair use guidelines for educational multimedia. Web teaching guide. Retrieved May 21, 2007, from http://www.dartmouth.edu/*webteach/articles/copyright. html.

Karjala, D., & Sugiyama, K. (1988). Fundamental concepts in Japanese and American copyright law. Retrieved May 27, 2007, from http://www.softic.or.jp/en/articles/Karjala-Sugiyama.html#

N_13_.

Kato, M. (1994). Chosakukenhou chikujyou kogi (Copyright case law studies). Tokyo: Chosakuken Jyouhou Center.

Malonis, J.A., (Ed.). (2002). Intellectual property. In Gale encyclopedia of E-commerce (Vol. 2, pp. 407–410). Detroit, OH: Gale.

Miller, S. (2004). Law and HCI. In William. Bainbridge (Ed.), Berkshire encyclopedia of human computer interaction (Vol. 1, pp. 413–420). Boston, MA: Berkshire.

Moore, S., (Ed.). (2005). Digital rights. The truth about the music business: A grassroots business andlegal guide. Boston, MA: ArtistPro Publishing.

Nunan, D. (1992). Research methods in language learning. Cambridge: Cambridge University Press.

Simons, J.D. (1995). Copyright law and video in the classroom. In C.P. Casanave & J.D. Simons (Eds.), Pedagogical perspectives on using films in foreign language classes (Keio University SFC Monograph #4). (pp.78–90). Fujisawa, Japan: Keio University SFC.

Simonson, M., Smaldino, S., Albright, M., & Zvacek, S. (2003). Teaching and learning at a distance. Upper Saddle River, NJ: Merrill Prentice Hall.

Simpson, C.A., (Ed.). (2005). Copyright for schools: A practical guide (4th, ed). Worthington, OH: Linworth Books.

Taylor, S.J., & Bogdan, R. (1984). Introduction to qualitative research methods (2nd ed). New York: John Wiley & Sons.

Warschauer, M. (1996). Computer-assisted language learning: An introduction. In S. Fotos (Ed.), Multimedia language teaching (pp. 3–20). Tokyo: Logos International.

Warschauer, M., & Meskill, C. (2000). Technology and second language learning. In J. Rosenthal (Ed.), Handbook of undergraduate second language education (pp. 303–318). Mahwah, NJ: Lawrence Erlbaum.

Wiersma, W. (1986). Research methods in education: An introduction (4th ed.). Newton, MA: Allyn & Bacon.

Witherspoon, J. (n.d.). e-learning: Ethics and governance considerations

Appendix
A survey about Japanese Copyright Laws

Please indicate which answer best applies to you. Questions marked with a * are required.

*1. Please indicate which applies to you: Native speaker of English. Native speaker of Japanese. Other:

*2. Have you ever read Japanese copyright laws? Yes. No. I have limited information of the laws Other:

*3. Have you ever participated in copyright law training seminars? Yes. No. I am not sure.

4. If 2 and 3 (above) do not apply to you, where do you obtain information about copyright laws? Mass media. Conversations with colleagues. Other:

Chapter 4

*5. Is it a violation of the law if you digitally reproduce commercial textbooks? Yes. No. I am not sure.

*6. How can you judge if materials are copyrighted or not? See if it has a copyright mark and a claim of 'Copyright reserved'. All publications and Internet materials are copyrighted if they are original. Other:

Computer Assisted Language Learning 179

Downloaded By: [Hiroshima Shudo University Library] At: 08:21 16 December 2008

*7. Have you ever shown videos or played CDs rented from a video/CD shop in class? Yes. No.

8. Is it a violation of the law to show rented videos, DVDs or CDs in class? Yes. No. I am not sure.

*9. Do you think downloading materials from the Internet for classroom use is a violation of copyright laws? Yes. No. I don't know.

*10. Is it a violation of the law to show programs recorded from television or the radio? Yes. No. I am not sure.

*11. Do you possess a fear of unintentionally violating copyright laws when you create CALL materials?

Very fearful Not at all fearful 4 3 2 1

*12. When producing or using materials for teaching and are unsure whether you are contravening copyright laws, what do you usually do? Ask lawyers or copyright law professionals. Investigate on the Internet or in the library. Make my own decision according to my existing knowledge of the law. Decide against producing the mate-

177

rials. Other:

13. Any other comments or ideas you have on this issue would be highly appreciated.

Chapter 5

Future Mobile Language Learning with VR and AR

Virtual Reality (VR) and Augmented Reality (AR) are technologies used to create an environment that does not actually exist. Such technology nowadays receives much attention and has been widely applied to various industries. However, the applications of VR/AR in education, especially in the language learning fields, are rarely, comprehensively and academically reported and reviewed. In this chapter, the authors first review the newest developments of VR ad AR technology, list the scattered experiences of using VR and AR seen from different sources, and then propose the possible use of the technology for language learning. Finally, the chapter will state the problems in integrating AR and VR with mobile language learning scenarios since most of AR and VR devices are mobile.

5.1. What is VR?

VR, short for Virtual Reality, is a combination of multiple technologies such as simulation, computer graphics, human-computer interfaces, sensor and multimedia. VR is actually a real-time, maginary created environment with which people can view, hear, smell or even physically sense.

As the marketplace value of the technology seems so promising,

IT giants such as Facebook and Google have started to invest huge funds in developing and employing VR technology for their services. Mark Zuckerberg, CEO of Facebook, asserted that reality is limited and is not fully satisfying, therefore needing to be extended to the virtual world. Part of the social interaction which currently takes place in realistic Facebook will likely soon be happening between avatars sharing a virtual world (Sulleyman, 2017).

Google chrome has already enabled users to view and interact with websites which have VR contents. Google users can follow links between pages and move between 2D and immersive viewing for VR-supported sites. 2016 was called the year of VR. The technology continued to attract attention in 2017.

5.2. What is AR?

AR is short for Augmented Reality. Different from VR, which is an environment totally virtual, Augmented Reality is a combination of virtual reality and existing environment. AR applications for smartphones typically include a global positioning system (GPS) to pinpoint the user's location and its compass to detect device orientation.

Pokémon Go, an extremely popular game around the world in 2016, was an AR application. The game uses the GPS ability to locate battle and exchange Pokémon, the virtual creatures.

As they did to VR, Facebook and Google also launched AR projects. Facebook introduced a new cross-platform camera interface which makes the camera the first augmented reality platform. Google's Tango project lets Tango become an augmented reality computing platform. The platform uses computer vision to enable handsets to detect their position relative to the world around them without using a GPS or other external signal. If the products are mature enough, the device can detect its surrounding just like human beings do.

5.3. AR/VR for General Educational Purpose

Using VR or AR, users can have realistic experiences with the 3D world and can even interact with it. For example, people can observe three-dimensional virtual objects in a 360 degree panorama using VR. With the help of AR, medical students can practice surgery in a controlled environment. AR is also widely used for navigation, sightseeing, system maintenance and product advertising.

Both VR and AR used to be mainly employed in digital games, but now have been used for various other purposes. Special devices to view VR content, such as the Oculus Rift Gear VR, which are called Head-Mounted Displays (HMD) are already available for ordinary people at reasonable prices. It can be predicted that AR and VR devices will become part of life in the same way that computers and televisions are now.

According to IDC (IDC, 2017), by 2020, there will be seven million AR and VR users around the world and will be at 20 times the market value in 2020 as it was in 2016.

There are two reasons that educational settings will soon witness a huge increase in AR/VR applications. Firstly, AR/ VR technology is in accord with educational theories of behaviorism and constructivism. Secondly,more and more VR/AR content is being created to be compatible with mobile phones - and mobile learning is becoming the main stream of e-learning (Wang, et.al. 2016). Jorge Martín-Gutiérrez. et.al. (2017) summarized the advantages of using virtual technologies: Virtual technologies increase students' motivation and engagement. Students immerse themselves in the virtual reality and feel as if protagonists; students are free to interact with virtual objects and other students; more and more VR/AR learning materials are now accessible via students' handsets such as smartphones which makes the learning environment ubiquitous.

Uimersiv is the largest platform in the world which provides VR educational content every month. After downloading the app for certain VR devices such as Gear VR, Oculus, Daydream…etc, users can learn about history, space or the human anatomy. Phenomena that can never be seen in reality are reproduced in VR and presented through VR devices. "Learn about Dinosaurs in VR", "A Journey into the Human Brain" , "Explore the International Space Station", "Explore Ancient Rome" are VR content for learners. Figure 1 shows dinosaurs in a virtual reality, a VR program that was launched by Uimersiv in July, 2017.

Chapter 5

Figure 1. Dinosaurs VR experience

Nearpod is an interactive presentation and assessment tool developed by an education company in the United States. The tool also provides VR resources. The company developed a VR course called College Tours, in which students can virtually visit the campus of famous universities around the world. Every lesson in the course was created using high-quality panoramic images with verbal narration, text, and study materials added. Figure 2 is an image taken from the lesson of "Visiting the University of Tokyo".

Figure 2. Nearpod VR: College Tours - Visiting University of Tokyo

Some other VR/AR learning contents may not be as well-known as Uimersiv and Nearpod, but still proves to be good practice for learning. Star Chart is a mobile app using AR for students to learn about constellations simply by aiming their phones towards the night sky. The app can provide students with virtual tours to many of the planets and the sun.

Thanks to VR/AR, when students touch a country map in a virtual globe placed in a class of world geography, the geographical information about the country will immediately display itself in a multimedia format. Earth AR is an AR app that lets students see the globe from different angles. The app can detect students' motion and respond with zoomed images. This app makes geography more interactive and engaging for students.

A student majoring in architecture can design models in a virtual world with the help of VR/AR applications. Instructions on machine operations can also be conducted in distance by using AR or VR. The situation of the work scene is transmitted to instructors in the distance, and the instructors guidance in texts or sound or images are delivered to the workers wearing AR or AR devices on the spot.

Many AR and VR applications have been used for tourism. An app called Boulevard can serve as a perfect example. Using this app, people can visit six of the world's best art museums without actually going there. In the app, visitors are able to interact with famous artworks and learn about the art.

5.4. AR/VR for Foreign Language Learning on Mobile Phones

Speaking. Learners can listen to conversations in the virtual world and interact with it. By moving bodies, learners can "go" to different places and "talk" to people at a place in the target languages. The following scene can be easily found in a typical VR language program: the learner "walks" out a hotel and wants to hail a taxi. Then a taxi comes and the driver asks him where he wants to go. A real-time conversation continues after the learner takes the taxi. When the taxi arrives at the airport, conversation will switch to a flight check-in.

These kinds of real-time speaking practices involving the participation of the learner obviously increases the learners' interest and lets them use the target language more effectively.

Mondly is such a VR app available for smartphones. Learners can have a chat with an online robot in the target language in a realistically authentic event. Instant feedback about the learner's pronunciation, grammar and vocabulary is quickly given by the app.

Figure 3. Role play in virtual conversations (image from "Learn Languages VR" by Mondly)

Vocabulary Study. Flashcards and closed tests are traditional ways to learn vocabulary in foreign language classes. Using a smartphone installed with an AR application the learner can learn vocabulary in a different, even a faster way. In an AR setting, when a learner places the smartphone camera on a particular object in a room, the name of the object and relative information will pop-up on the smartphone's screen. See figure 4 as an example.

Figure 4. Learning vocabulary in VR (image from "Learn English in VR – Language VR app)

Santos. Et.al.(2016) reports an experiment using AR to learn English vocabulary. They divided the learners into two groups. One group learned vocabulary with the AR app, while the other group learned the same vocabulary with traditional flashcards. The experiment shows that using AR can reduce cognitive load, improve attention, and increase satisfaction.

Reading. If those difficult sentences, paragraphs or even passages are presented in AR or VR for readers to see, to touch or to feel, then the text can surely become much easier and more impressive for the readers to understand. In Figure 5, several difficult pages describing dinosaurs in the book were made into markers. In AR, markers are usually regular images or small objects which were created and trained beforehand for cameras to recognize. When the camera of a smartphone or a tablet PC is placed over a marker, readers will see virtual 3D animated dinosaurs.

Figure 5. Display AR information on a tablet PC (image captured from Jurassic AR Book)

Experiencing cultural differences. AR/VR is very helpful in helping students experience cultural differences. By using AR or VR contents, without going abroad, students can vividly learn the history of foreign countries, visit a tourist spot thousands miles away, walk on a campus of a foreign university and even "stay" with a host family. Hastings & Brunotte (2017) reported that a smartphone-based VR program could reduce the anxiety associated with study abroad.

Chapter 5

5.5. Problems and Limitations of VR and AR for Foreign Language Learning

Applying AR /VR technology to foreign language education has just commenced. The technology will become popular in various educational scenarios in the near future. However, problems and limitations still exist.

Firstly, in order to create the VR/AR learning content, teachers will need to invest in hardware and software. For example, if a teacher wants to create a 360-degree video, then a spherical camera with 360-degree lens is needed. When a 2D video is converted to a 3D video, special software like Media Converter becomes necessary. Furthermore, even though an existing VR learning content is available for use, sometimes a user needs to wear a special HMD to view it – many VR contents cannot be well-perceived by the naked eye.

Secondly, the threshold to create AR and VR learning content is high and beyond the reach of many teachers without the necessary technical background. To shoot 360 degree VR videos needs certain video-taking skills; to write the interface codes, a knowledge of 3D-modeling, programming languages like C/C++/C# and software development kits (SDKs) is needed; for better design, experience in 3D production is preferable (Herrera, 2017). In addition, a huge amount of time needs to be guaranteed to produce and test VR/AR learning materials.

Thirdly, as AR/VR technology is still in its infancy, trends and standards have been changing. A learning VR or AR content created

189

today may not be compatible with devices emerging tomorrow.

Fourthly but not finally, the pedagogical theories for VR/AR use in education are not well developed. Research papers till the present on AR/VR for learning, particularly for language learning, are still extremely few. In practice, teachers may feel frustrated when they are not able to find any pedagogical theories to follow nor any previously successful examples to which to refer.

5.6. Conclusion

After introducing the definitions of VR and AR, this paper has reviewed the latest developments of the technology and its current applications in industry as well as in general education settings. In order to fill the gap of research on the use of VR/AR for language learning purposes, the paper has discussed the possible applications of existing VR/AR products for foreign language speaking, vocabulary study, reading and cultural difference exploration. Although VR/AR for language learning is very promising for language teachers and learners, the hurdle to use the technology is still high due to the fact that VR/AR learning content creation is very technically demanding.

(This capter was originally published in *Journal of the Center for Foreign Language Education, Shimane University. No.13*, 27-33 with Jun Iwata)

Reference

Augeri, T. (2017). The Prospects for VR/AR in Geographic Education and Research. Retrieved from https://vrvoice.co/prospects-vrar-geographic-education-research/ on January 2, 2018.

Hastings & Brunotte (2017). Reducing Study abroad Anxiety through Smartphone Virtual Reality.*JALTCALL 2017 Conference Proceedings*. P48

IDC (2017). Worldwide Quarterly Augmented and Virtual Reality Headset Tracker. Retrieved from https://www.idc.com/tracker/showproductinfo.jsp?prod_id=1501 on January 2, 2017

Herrera, E. (2017). How you can become an AR/VR developer. Retrieved from https://blog.pusher.com/how-you-can-become-an-ar-vr-developer/ on January 2, 2018.

Martín-Gutiérrez, J., Efrén Mora, C., Añorbe-Díaz, B., González-Marrero, A. (2017). Virtual Technologies Trends in Education. *EURASIA Journal of Mathematics Science and Technology Education*. 13(2), 469-486.

Nagamura (2016). A Prospect of AR/VR Technology. Technical Report of Mitsubushi Research Institute, Inc. http://www.mri.co.jp/opinion/column/tech/tech_20160520.html

Santos, M.E.C., Lübke, A.., Taketomi, T. et al. RPTEL (2016) 11: 4. https://doi.org/10.1186/s41039-016-0028-2

Sulleyman, A. (2017). Mark Zuckerberg says virtual reality is better than the 'limited' real world. Retrieved from http://www.independent.co.uk/life-style/gadgets-and-tech/news/mark-zuckerberg-virtual-reality-better-real-world-comments-vr-a7995546.html

Wang, et al. (2016). Learning via Mobile Phones – Students Learning Styles, Needs, Preferences and Concerns *International Journal of Innovation and Learning*. Vol.19 ,pp.431-443

Author Profile

Shudong Wang, Ph.D., is an Associate Professor in the Academic Assembly, Institute for the Promotion of Education and Research, Shimane University, Japan. His research interests include educational technology and applied linguistics. He has published widely in the fields of computer assisted language learning and mobile assisted language learning. Some of his papers have been included in leading journals in educational technology such as The British Journal of Educational Technology, Language Learning and Technology and Computer Assisted Language Learning.

He has led or joined several e-learning projects financed by grants from the Ministry of Education, Culture, Sports, Science and Technology of Japan. His most recent project is to build a mobile learning system to help foreigners in Japan with disaster prevention and preparedness.

Mobile Phones for Language Learning in Japanese Universities

2019 年 8 月 5 日　第 1 刷発行

著　者　Shudong Wang

発行人　大杉　剛

発行所　株式会社 風詠社
　　　　〒553-0001　大阪市福島区海老江 5-2-2
　　　　　　　　　　大拓ビル 5 - 7 階
　　　　℡ 06（6136）8657　http://fueisha.com/

発売元　株式会社 星雲社
　　　　〒112-0005　東京都文京区水道 1-3-30
　　　　℡ 03（3868）3275

装幀　2 DAY

印刷・製本　小野高速印刷株式会社

©Shudong Wang 2019, Printed in Japan.

ISBN978-4-434-26387-3 C3082

乱丁・落丁本は風詠社宛にお送りください。お取り替えいたします。